THE
BREATH
OF
GOD

—

by Swami Chetanananda

THE BREATH OF GOD

—

by Swami Chetanananda

Rudra Press • Cambridge, Massachusetts

Rudra Press
P.O. Box 1973
Cambridge, Massachusetts 02238

Cover and Text Design: Leslie Goldstein
Cover Photograph: Lucille Handberg
Photograph of Author: Patty Slote

Manufactured in the United States of America

ISBN: 0-915801-05-1

Grateful acknowledgement is made to Beacon Press (Boston)
for permission to reprint the poem on page xv from *The Kabir Book*
by Robert Bly, copyright © 1971, 1977 by Robert Bly, © 1977 by
The Seventies Press. Reprinted by permission of Beacon Press.
Grateful acknowledgement is also made to the Frank Lane Photo
Agency (London) for permission to reprint the cover photograph,
taken by Lucille Handberg of a tornado near Jasper, Minnesota
on July 8, 1927.

iv

Come to the semma

come, come again –

even if you have broken your vows

a thousand times,

come, come again.

Ours is not a caravan

of despair.

—

(Adapted from the words
Jalalu'ddin Rumi had carved over the gateway
to his spiritual community.)

CONTENTS

Are you looking for me?
I am in the next seat.
My shoulder is against yours.
You will not find me in stupas,
not in Indian shrine rooms,
nor in synagogues, nor in cathedrals:
not in masses, nor kirtans, not in legs
winding around your own neck, nor in eating
nothing but vegetables.
When you really look for me,
you will see me instantly —
you will find me in the tiniest house of time.
Kabir says: Student, tell me, what is God?
He is the breath
inside the breath.

—

KABIR

PREFACE

———

When I talked with Swami Chetanananda about writing this preface, I said, "I haven't studied with you as long as many of your other students. The most I can do is write about things I've noticed during the time I've worked with you." He said, "That doesn't matter. The things you notice, even after a short time, are the same things you'll continue to notice over the years. It's just that at different moments you'll understand them in different ways."

I first heard Swamiji* at the Sunday morning public program held at the Nityananda Institute, where he is the abbot. Having arrived several minutes late, I was

———

* The term "Swami" refers to his being an initiate of the Saraswati monastic order of India, and means "master of oneself." "Ji" is a term of love and respect.

seated in a far corner. I couldn't see him well over the heads of the people in front of me, and so my initial impressions grew from listening to him. More than anything else, I noticed the directness and the simplicity with which he spoke. Indeed, submerged as I had been for years in the academic lecture style of the university, I was at first tempted to dismiss what he was saying. It seemed too ordinary. Too much like common sense.

I should add that I had, for some years, also felt leery of Americans involved in Indian religious traditions and practices, assuming that they must be the watering-down of something authentic. I came prepared to be unimpressed. I was therefore struck by the response of my companion, a visiting professor from India. "This could be my *guru* in India sitting with his students," he said. "The whole feeling is the same."

On that particular occasion, Swamiji happened to be responding to people's questions about raising children. Despite my prejudices, what he said kept making me nod. Somewhat to my surprise, I found myself thinking about his remarks repeatedly during the weeks that followed. I returned, and became a student at the Institute.

I continue to notice his use of language. I notice especially that every time I think I have his words pinioned, they suddenly quicken and take flight, soaring over what he's just said and seeing it from a different sky. Going beyond themselves, still they retain the appearance of simplicity, just as the flight of the bird seems simple.

Another way to put this would be to say that what Swamiji expresses is neither prose nor philosophy, although it overlaps with both. Rather, he expresses a kind of embodied poetry. Remember that poetry turns language around, putting things together in unexpected ways in order to break you into a new way of seeing things – a new way of being. Poetry confronts you with paradox and contradiction, teasing you to re-think your more conventional assumptions. It is an experience through which the words try to lead you. Listening to and being with Swamiji are both something like that.

In what way? In one breath, he may be laying out the highly sophisticated complex of the tradition he teaches, taking texts so condensed that they verge on being opaque, and, in a manner both intent and casual, bringing them into the territory of lived experience. In the next breath, he may be talking about fishing – not theoretically, but with the expertise of the practiced angler. Then, just as you're trying to get your mind around that, he may refer to developments in the current commodities market, tease you about your exaggerated attachment to some aspect of your own self-importance, tell you something about a piece of primitive or Asian art that interests him (and about which he is expert), quote a snatch of the poetry of Rumi or Kabir, and get up to put on a song by the Talking Heads – all of it done simply and naturally.

The mind-breaker in this involves going beyond your own assumptions of what a spiritual teacher is supposed to be. For example, one assumption is the idea that a spiritual teacher no longer has any connection to ordinary life as most of us live it. Going beyond this assumption involves thinking about how there might exist some state beyond the seeming contradictions and paradoxes, as well as thinking about how to experience that state yourself.

A spiritual teacher is a kind of shape-shifter. He or she is utterly ordinary, and yet ordinary in no way at all. A teacher invests the most mundane of experiences with the recognition that it too, is another expression of the essence of Life Itself. I remember one time when Swamiji and I were talking about writing. I had just told him about an exercise that involved a process of free-association. He thought about it for a moment, then said, apologetically, "I'm afraid I'm rather boring. I look at everything and see only one thing – the Self."

I notice how Swamiji looks at things and at people. When I was younger, I had an intuition that a certain kind of profound communication took place when all the veils were stripped from two people's eyes, and they looked at each other out of a truth that couldn't be spoken. From working with Swamiji, I now understand somewhat better what I was then trying to express in an inchoate way. When someone else sees you, and recognizes everything that you are, then it goes beyond "I," "you," or "we," and something holy happens.

I have noticed both in myself and others a process of healing, which is an expression of communion with the teacher. It takes the form of the most obvious, as well as the most subtle, transformations. On the more visible level, as people learn to still their minds and to go beyond the stresses and tensions of daily living, they free up their energy and can begin to explore their own potential in new directions. Their health improves, they begin to look their best, and they find that things which used to seem insurmountable have extraordinary ways of resolving themselves. People take on a new lightness and humor, and discover that they can, in fact, undertake those things that they had always wanted to do with their lives. There's a kind of magic in it which, at the same time, is utterly ordinary. Things just happen.

It has occurred to me that one of the things that enables a person to grow in this way is the sense of being recognized while still in the wasteland of denials and excuses. This recognition brings with it a sense of being loved anyway, and of being invited – at your own pace – to drop the excuses and to live instead in the heartland of a much deeper sense of vitality and joy. In the midst of all your evasions, Swamiji has a way of looking at you and saying, "Remember, this is me you're talking to."

Of course, there are two sides to being recognized. On the one hand, there's the side of, "Oh God, the blinders, the backdrops, and the camouflage don't work. I've been found out!" On the other hand, there's the side of, "Oh God, finally somebody sees and acknowledges who and what I really am." Gradually, the excuses begin to disintegrate, like playhouses constructed by children from cardboard and glue. Then you see that home is actually a much bigger place. A person can live in playhouses only so long.

Swamiji might tell me that I've dwelt too much on personality in talking about him – that is, on the aspect of the teacher he considers to be the least important. I may have. Yet there is some method to it. It is an oblique way of trying to say something about the Self – about how It expresses Itself through one particular person; about what it's like to be around the transcendent in the commonplace; about what it's like to know someone who addresses you with such compassion, love, and trust that you discover you do, indeed, have the courage to walk through your fear. Perhaps most of all, it's a way of saying something about what it's like to work with a spiritual teacher.

Working with Swamiji occasionally makes me think about the stories of teachers I heard as I was growing up — among them, the stories of Jesus. I've thought of the stories about how the people who went with him made the choice to do so — people like Simon and Andrew. I imagine that one day they stood casting their nets at the edge of the Sea of Galilee, the ropes of the net chafing their hands calloused from years of labor. Maybe the wind rose from time to time, blowing the spray and the sunlight in their teeth. Suddenly they looked up and noticed a stranger standing at the edge of the water. He must have looked at them, and something about his presence awoke something dormant in them. They dropped their nets and their plans, left their boats and all the ambitions that had sailed them, and cast themselves out onto a new and knowing sea. In doing so, they became what they had always been — fishermen — but in a new way. In that encounter with Jesus as a man and as a teacher, I suspect that wanting to be with him and to study with him seemed the most natural thing to do. I suspect, too, that the students of the Buddha or of Lao-tzu must have had like experiences.

Over the years, I wondered what it might have been like to meet someone who demonstrated the meaning of being human in the fullest sense. Someone in whom you recognized the essence of what you had always longed for, even when you forgot that you were longing for it. Someone whose way of being reminded you that you had never quite stopped listening for the overtones of that essence in the heart of every event — even though you had also spent years closing your ears when you heard it because it was too painfully sweet and the longing for it seemed likely to break your heart. Someone who was telling you that with practice, training, and devotion, you could find your entire life to be the experience and the expression of that very essence. This is the gift that the teacher shows you is always present within you, waiting.

I once asked Swamiji if a teacher ever took time off from being a teacher. He said no. At that point, I realized that I had imported yet one more assumption from all my other experiences of education. Swamiji's response made it clear that a teacher is a teacher simply by virtue of being what he or she is. To think of it otherwise is like saying, "Can you stop being yourself at five o'clock?"

A teacher isn't an academic whose concern must be to convey the intellectual understanding of a body of concepts. Instead, he or she teaches what it is to *be* and to *live* in the continuous experience of the Self. This means that there is never a moment when the teacher isn't teaching. This may, at some points, find expression in texts, but authentic learning in this case really involves the student's experience of the teacher and the experience of one's own Self that this promotes. This is the more subtle learning that occurs.

In this sense, the teacher isn't someone who sets out to be a teacher at all. Rather, he or she is someone in whom other people recognize something so compelling that, to varying degrees, they alter their own lives to be around it. The teacher makes the choice to respond to this. In the Buddhist tradition, the *bodhisattva* is the enlightened person who delays his or her own departure from the world because of a commitment not to leave until all other beings have also reached enlightenment. It is an ultimate expression of compassion and generosity. There is, as I think, much of this in what any real teacher does.

Different teachers find themselves responding to different traditions as the most adequate vehicle in which to convey their own experience and understanding. Swamiji teaches in the tradition of the *Kula* school of Kashmir Shaivism, a tradition which has its origins in northwest India and dates back many centuries. His teacher was Swami Rudrananda, known as Rudi, who was also an American meditation master in this tradition. When Rudi passed away in 1973, Swamiji took on the direction of the various groups of Rudi's students.

Rudi's teacher had been Swami Nityananda, a holy man of India recognized by many as a saint, who was also the teacher of Swami Muktananda. It was Swami Muktananda who initiated Swamiji into the Saraswati monastic order in 1978 as an acknowledgement of Swamiji's understanding of the tradition.

At the heart of this tradition is the process of coming to be aware of the inner Self, which is the essence of all things and of Life Itself. Through the practice of meditation and of working with the teacher, a student learns to still the mind and begins to discern the continuous presence of the Self within. This practice and the understanding that emerges from it inform all of Swamiji's teaching, and are illustrated in the talks included in this book.

What follows are excerpts from talks given by Swamiji in two different settings. On Sunday mornings, Swamiji sits with students and visitors to the Institute, and responds to their questions about the meditation practice that he teaches. At that time, people are invited to raise whatever questions they might have. Secondly, after teaching *kundalini yoga* classes in the evening, Swamiji sometimes gives short talks. The selections in this book are drawn from both settings, and span the period from January to June of 1987.

In reading them, you will notice that they follow something of a random order. This is for several reasons. The first of these is that when grouped by topic, they tend to appear systematic and formal in a way inconsistant with Swamiji's overall approach. Moreover, one loses the more subtle distinctions between pieces on similar topics.

Many of the pieces are responses to a given individual, addressed to that person's level of understanding and experience of the practice. This makes for a multitonal coverage of a variety of topics. Think of each one, then, not as a single note, but as higher and lower, finer and slower frequencies that, when taken together, create a chord that resonates from a central idea.

Furthermore, when you study with Swamiji you also hear him circle around similar topics on more than one occasion. It is in the layering and overlayering of his responses that your own understanding deepens. You notice the same things, but understand them differently. This book is an attempt to convey something about the experience of that, and of what it's like to be in the company of a teacher.

Linda L. Barnes
Editor

ALL THINGS ARE
NOTHING MORE

——

All things are nothing more than condensations of the
creative energy of Life.

AS AN ICEBERG FLOATING
IN THE OCEAN

———

God and the Self are one. If you think about God as separate from the Self, then the problem is this: you tend to think, "I'm small and God is great. This means that I'm locked into my own smallness. Something must be missing in me."

This is a source of great misunderstanding. God dwells within you always. Furthermore, if you look carefully within yourself at the in-dwelling Lord, you'll discover that you are nothing but *that* – that your body is nothing but a coalescing of that divine, creative power. It's like ice and water. Ice is water in which the heat is reduced, the vibration of the molecules diminishes, and the molecules themselves take on a solid, crystallized form.

As an iceberg floating in the ocean is separated only by degrees of vibration from its fundamental reality, so are you only a crystallization of the Divine. The iceberg floating on the ocean might think of itself as separate, but in reality it has come from the ocean, and to the ocean it will return. When that inner energy is re-awakened and its entire vibration changed, then the ice melts, and the divine essence that you are becomes apparent.

Assume that it's all there within you, and that you're within it all. Is this so hard to understand? Go to the ocean, take a bucket of water from the shore, and pour it back into the ocean. Then, find that bucket of water once more. Where did it go? Show me which is separate – find even a single drop of it. You don't talk about waves as being separate from the ocean. It is simply the nature of the ocean to have them. Nor do you give each of them a name. Waves arise and subside faster than you can say Chetanananda. So it is with you. You arise and subside quickly – just like that – out of, and back into, the Divine.

When you stop praying for what you think is missing, and simply attune yourself to the extraordinary richness, the quality, and the love that are at the core of your heart, then the ocean itself becomes apparent, and all the rest is just the debris that floats on the surface. Like all debris, it is dead. The ocean is what is alive.

THE ESSENCE OF ALL LIFE
IS ONE THING

———

The most important thing for you to understand is that, despite the appearance of multiplicity, the essence of all Life is really only one thing. If you think about this, then whenever you get in a tight spot, you're not going to fight it. You're going to surrender. "Surrender," in this case, doesn't mean that you're going to give up. Rather, it means that first you're going to relax. Then, the inner flow of Life Itself is going to rise up, poke you on the shoulder, and say, "Here I am." And you'll say, "There you are." From that point, all difficulties can be overcome. It's the thought of "Oh, I'm all alone. I'm separate and isolated in this world, and I have to struggle against other people for everything I want," that causes great misunderstanding. That's the beginning of the downward path.

The direct experience of the unity of all things is available to each and every human being. You need only look into your own heart. Of course, if you do so after not having looked for a long time, then your heart may not be all that open, and you may not sense the experience of unity for a while. If I were your friend, and you hadn't called me in six months, do you think I would be immediately cheery and responsive when I first heard from you? I'd probably say, "Where have you been?"

It's really quite extraordinary to see the degree to which what happens in the heart governs your entire experience of the world. When the heart is open, you feel wonderful, you're kind to people, and good things happen. When it's closed, whatever happens seems awful. This means that the heart dominates your whole experience.

You have to spend some time with your own heart. Every day, preserve some spot in the day just to sit or lie down. Start out by feeling your heart beating. Then, breathe into that area, and feel the breath going into your heart. Every breath you take will dissolve another layer of tension, and reveal another layer of the beauty that is in you all the time. If you think about that every day and spend a little time with it, then it will always be there for you. You may forget it when you're busy moving around, but it will always be there for you to build on. With practice, it will continue to open and reveal to you all that you are. This brings not only the understanding, but also the experience that all life is really only one thing.

OPENING THE HEART

———

Change is based upon the depth of contact you have with your total environment. When I use the term "opening the heart," this is simply a way of talking about the degree to which you participate in this total environment. It is also a way of talking about the amount of energy you're absorbing, as well as the amount of change you're facilitating within yourself and, consequently, within the environment itself. It is a reciprocal event. What is outside of you comes in, and what is inside of you comes out.

This is a dynamic process. The more you're aware of it and the less you resist it, the more you grow. The degree to which you resist it is the degree to which you are certain to have emotional and, ultimately, serious physical impediments. It's not necessary, in the long term, to identify the source or the cause of your resistance. On the one hand, there can be any number of causes that will look like a hundred thousand different things, and you can call them anything you want. On the other hand, you don't have to name them at all. In fact, the minute you name them, you limit your ability to respond to them. It's only important to note that resistance exists, and to begin to deal with it directly.

EVEN PAIN IS NOT
A PROBLEM

———

When you come into this world, you have no problems. The initial purity, which gave rise to your life in the first place, simply *is*. Moreover, that same purity sustains you throughout your life. Never is it gone, nor does it ever abandon you. It's only that you forget about it and then, at that point, the idea of problems arises.

This means that there's really no such thing as problems. Even pain is not a problem. (You will realize this when you reach the point of being able to accept the pain in your life.) What's more amazing than that is that the abundance of power which created the whole universe is the same power which gives you life. Only because of notions such as "problems" and "pain" do you deny the experience of the purity and power un-folding within yourself.

The abundance of that purity and power is beyond anything you can imagine. Therefore, to think that there is an absence of anything in your life – and so, some problem – becomes ridiculous. If the same resource that created the whole universe is within you, then how can anything be missing? The way we say it is that the Self has no problems.

TENSION

The science of *kundalini yoga* is a twofold science: it is a science of the structure of the energy within you, as well as a science of the structure and flow of the energy around you. These two sides – inner and outer – are intimately, reciprocally linked. They feed each other, and only when you master both sides do you have a complete understanding of the oneness of Life Itself.

In the exploration of this science, the fundamental skill you must develop is that of dealing with tension. What is tension? Tension is powerful energy. It, too, has an internal and an external component, both of which are intimately related. There is never a time when the tensions outside you aren't connected to tensions inside you – even when you aren't aware of feeling tense.

When you encounter tensions outside, there is never a time that you can't stop and ask yourself, "What did I do to cause this?"

I'm certain that you can recall experiences of tension that you have handled successfully. In such cases, the energy of that moment becomes part of the whole energy field that you are. This then increases the entire level of your own energy and of your power, if you want to put it that way. I'm sure that you also have less pleasant recollections of times when you mishandled the tensions you encountered and, as a result, landed sitting down. Such experiences severely reduce your energy level.

There are two critical skills to learn when handling tension, and the main one of these is learning to be open. As tensions arise or as you encounter them, you must have the control within yourself not to get entangled in them. Instead of becoming polarized by the situation, you must have the self-mastery to open, and to feel the flow of energy within yourself. As you do this, you must draw in the tension, absorb it, and digest it. This is because tension is nothing but energy that has become crystallized. Your openness dissolves that crystallization, allowing the energy to become part of the total flow of energy that you are. As you open and absorb this different kind of chemistry, a shift happens.

This brings us to the second skill. It is out of the shift which occurs that you speak. You must learn to speak carefully, in a way that allows this flow of energy – this tension which you have incorporated as energy into your own field – to become integrated into your approach to the situation. The alternative is to regurgitate all the stupidities that kept a stupid situation rolling on in a stupid way in the first place.

Instead, you must take the energy you've absorbed and channelled, and re-express it in a way that uplifts the situation. Then, the change that has happened in you allows for a change in the total energy field that surrounds you and of which you are part. This change manifests itself as a higher level of understanding, and as a generally more positive expression on your part and on the part of all concerned.

It is natural that this should happen. If you've really connected to this energy and done your work, then you have changed within yourself. That change in you should naturally flow outward and be articulated as a change in the whole event. It can't help but be this way. If Einstein's theory of relativity is right, this is the only thing that can take place. Because you have changed, then the situation must change.

This presents you with two choices. The first is to resist growing. After all, human beings do not evolve naturally. Repeatedly we allow the lowest level of stupidity in any environment to magnetize and orient us. Our capacity to take on the crystallization of every kind of tension, and to make it our own, is vast. Almost nobody – and I mean nobody – understands how to dissolve even the tensions within themselves, let alone any other kind of tension. But, if you are really going to grow, it is essential to learn how to do this. Indeed, this *is* the second of the two choices.

The tensions that you encounter within yourself and around you represent the opportunity to expand and refine the energy field that you are – to refine it to the extent that you begin to appreciate the subtle and profound connections between the inner and the outer. Without this refinement, it's impossible to have the sensitivity, the insight, or the understanding it takes to make these connections.

You will always be facing tensions. If it's not one thing, it's another – the tensions of your particular cultural perspective, your family background, your biological imperatives, or your racial, sexual, and ethnic orientations. All of these can cause you to have a contracted identification of who and what you are.

However, the lowest common denominator with which we identify ourselves is the assumption that all we are is "I," with "my" needs: "Gimme this, gimme that, what about my need for this, and what about my thing over there?" This ability to reduce ourselves to the *mantra* of stupidity – "What's going to happen to me?" – profoundly inhibits our capacity to grow. The more we identify ourselves in this way, the more the life flow in us is reduced to the lowest level of energy that exists in any environment. If we are to realize our full potential and our true identity in the Absolute, we must release every last one of our identifications with these tensions.

This brings us to the alternative choice: always to learn, to make an effort, and to do the tedious and taxing work of taking in tensions and of promoting change and refinement within and around us. This we work at every day, step by step, by treating every person we encounter with love and respect.

Now you might think, this is a clinker! Where did he come up with this new thing about love and respect? When I say that the fundamental thing is love and respect, I mean that the fundamental expression of love and respect involves learning how to deal with tensions – both your own and those of other people. This is a practical, powerful expression of real love and respect. As you cultivate this love and respect, you are developing a powerful self-mastery, which you articulate in your genuine capacity to serve other human beings.

If you want to look at it another way, Jesus once said, "No greater love hath a person than to lay down his life for his friends." For you to deny your own narrow identification with the constraints of tension while you take on another person's tension – or at least deal with your own – is the greatest demonstration of both sacrifice and service. It is a service that is at once of immediate benefit to the person you serve, and even more, to you yourself.

This process ignites and is part of a tremendous fire within us – a fire of love. This is not a fire of romance; nor is it a fire of sweetness, light, and joy. It is a serious fire which will burn up your guts and every single tension inside of you and, in doing so will, at the same time, liberate the creative potential and the deepest understanding hidden within you. The effort that you make within yourself while sitting in meditation should be one of connecting with that energy and of facing your own resistance to doing so. But this alone is not enough. You must

14

then take your experience of this, and translate it into a total life experience.

Understand this: how you deal with tensions — your own and the tensions you encounter in the world — is really the fulcrum point. It is the linchpin. It is a daily demonstration of your self-control and your self-mastery. It is a daily articulation of your understanding of service, of love, and of respect. It is a daily manifestation of your connection to God. Finally, it is a no-jive, down-to-earth, real-life happening that you undertake every single day. In this effort of consuming tensions lies the nourishment and the fuel necessary for the total transformation that you ask for.

I am not the transformation. *That* is the transformation. I'm just the keeper of the fire. If the flue gets clogged with soot, I clean it out. If the fire dies down, I bank it up. If you get lost in the process, I make sure you get found again. When you work at being open, you do get lost. It's easy to become so fascinated by openness, and by the effort it takes to get there, that you forget about where you were going or what it was you started out to do. It's my job to point you back in the right direction.

But, in the long run, you're the one who has to learn how to be open without getting lost. You have to remember who you are and where you're going, in the context of this inner effort you make to remain open. This is necessary so that the energy you absorb and consume, and the expansion that results, will re-articulate themselves in your life in concrete, practical, and beneficial ways which will serve you and all the people to whose lives you are connected. Only in this way will you really learn about energy – about the subtle energy of Life Itself.

The point I want you to remember is this: serving God is consuming tensions.

BREATHING IS FREE

Whenever you find negative reactions to things building up, you can respond either by becoming tense, or by breathing in and out, deeply and smoothly. Breathe in and out for about four or five minutes, and be aware of your breathing. This will dissolve the negativity. Every time it starts to build up a little, take a few minutes to become aware of your breathing again. This is a simple thing, but if you've ever sat and done it, you know that it feels wonderful to breathe. If you feel your breath for even a little while, it becomes hard to be negative about anything.

It's amazing that the fundamental things we need to live are free. They are simple, and quite beautiful. You require nothing to get at them or to understand them. Nobody has to give you permission or approval for you to have them. It's all quite simple. This is not the same as saying that it's easy, however. In a real way, life is a lot of work, and there is no reason to be terribly optimistic about it. Yet the issue here isn't whether or not you are optimistic; rather, it is how you feel about what you do, and the level at which you participate in that.

Life is always going to be work, and there will always be some pain associated with it. Still, the basic resources you require to rise above that pain, and to allow your life to be an expression of much more than the sum of all the painful components – those resources are free and present now. They are always present. So, be neither negative nor optimistic. Just be joyous in whatever it is that life requires you to do.

STAGES IN PRACTICE

The first stage in your practice of *kundalini yoga* is one that requires a concentrated, conscious effort to learn to feel the *chakras* (the energy centers) within you, to breathe into them and feel them expand, and to feel the flow of energy that goes down through them and then up your spinal column. This flow – which passes down the front of your body and up the back – forms a circuit of energy. This circuit has always been there – you simply cultivate your awareness of it through practice. This is another way of saying that you make the concentrated, conscious effort every day to open your mind and your heart. Your effort allows the energy to work its way through you completely, and to nourish every part of you.

The second stage is one of intense, concentrated awareness. You could also say that because you have made a consistent, concentrated, conscious effort, you come to have an intense awareness of the energy pulsating and vibrating within you. You experience this energy as the essence of your mind, your senses, your emotions, and your physical body. It is the essence of all your thoughts, all your feelings, and all your actions.

The third stage is the one of a pure, concentrated relaxation. It is a release of all effort and of all remembrance, in which there is simply pure awareness. At this stage, you experience everything as nothing but waves of your own creative Self. There is no other. There is only one.

As you work, you will experience each of these three stages, even from the beginning. However, during your everyday life, one or the other will predominate. In the beginning, it's one thing; in the middle, it changes; and, finally, there is nothing but one thing – the recognition that your own inner Self is pure creativity. It is the one creativity which has given rise to everything and to all experience. It is at this stage that true success is attained.

Realize that success is not measured by the amount of money you make, or by the amount of recognition you achieve. Rather, success is the degree to which you mobilize the resources within yourself, and the degree to which you allow these resources to manifest. This is success. It is also fulfillment.

THE BREATH INSIDE
THE BREATH

Chakras are nerve centers, which you experience when
your system is highly energized. Although they are not
exactly physical, we experience their energy in an extremely tangible way. For instance, when you've had a
powerful emotional experience, your throat may feel
blocked. In moments of extreme anger, the point two fingers below your navel may become completely con-
stricted. If your heart is closed to something, you may
feel unbearable anguish, while at other times, your
heart suddenly opens, and you experience a feeling of
total joy and well-being. It is our experience of the
energy of these *chakras* that determines our state of mind
and our behavior.

There are three primary nerves in the body which have to do with this. The first of these is called the *shushumna*, which is the central spinal column. On either side of the *shushumna* are two other primary nerves: the *ida* and the *pingala*. These crisscross back and forth. At the points where the three cross each other, you have the primary *chakras*. There are actually many, many *chakras*, but in our practice we focus on the seven primary ones. These are located at the base of your spine, at the base of your sex, in your abdomen, about two fingers below your navel, in your heart, at your throat, between your eyes, and at the top of your head. The solar plexus is also a *chakra* in some systems. *Kundalini yoga* is simply the practice by which you cultivate your awareness of these *chakras*, and of the energy flow within them.

Through practice, we feel the flow of energy down the front of our body through the *chakras*, and then up the spinal column to the top of the head. This is a circuit. We don't create this circuit – it already exists. It simply is. We just work to cultivate our awareness of it. In the process of doing this, we gradually withdraw our attention from the physical world. When we take our attention inside, we become attuned to the energy which is the support of the physical world. This slowly changes our whole awareness of ourselves, and our understanding of all experience. We begin to understand ourselves and all other people as nothing but energy flows. Then, we come to understand all of life and all experience to be nothing but an expression of conscious energy. This awareness changes how we feel about ourselves, and completely rearranges our priorities.

Twelve times a minute, every minute, day after day, a pulsation flows up the length of the spinal column. Because it happens twelve times a minute, that's why there's some continuity in our appearance. Actually, we're all like movies, but the frames – in this case, the pulsations – move so fast that we don't notice it's a new frame each time. This goes on as long as we're alive.

Your own breath – that is, the breathing you're usually aware of – is nothing more than the gross manifestation of the pulsation through the cerebrospinal fluid. What is amazing is that this pulsation is the same as the pulsation of all that is.

Let me put it a little differently. The Breath of Life – this pulsation – moves through your spinal column twelve times a minute. The breath that you're usually aware of is nothing more than the gross manifestation of this pulsation. It's like going outside on a cold winter day, and having your breath take form so that you can see it. That's what we are. We're nothing more than a form taken on briefly by the Breath of God. That is why we practice focusing on our breathing – to become aware of and to understand the flow of this breath inside our breath.

You see, there is only one thing behind the appearance of many things, and that one thing is the energy of Life Itself. The energy of Life – the basic pulsation in all things – is really nothing but pure consciousness, or pure awareness. This pure awareness is both infinite and vital. It must be vital because awareness without vitality would be essentially inert, and we know from our own experience that life is not inert.

In the process of displaying its vitality, this infinite awareness pulsates. Its pulsations vibrate at different rates, giving rise to the appearance of different forms, but without diminishing that infinite awareness in any way. It isn't as if something is subtracted from it in order to give rise to forms – that is, to the manifestations of all experience. It is all still one thing. There is always really only one thing, one Self.

This Self – this vital consciousness – is also an infinitely *creative* energy. Its main characteristic is complete freedom – the capacity to change. Each of us is nothing more than a limited extension of it – one way in which the creative energy articulates its potentiality. This means that our essential nature is one of complete freedom. The final goal of all our practice to feel the *chakras* and the flow is to have a perfect understanding of this: to become aware that we are really everything that is. Then there is nothing we have to change; nothing we have to do. There is no place to go. There is only knowing yourself – knowing the Self.

IN THE PRACTICE OF MEDITATIVE TECHNIQUES

———

We talk about meditative techniques to give you something on which to focus your mind when you start to experience fear or resistance. Both fear and resistance are reactions to the presence of a strong energy, and both indicate the presence of a strong energy. Often, people react to energy of this kind by closing their hearts, tightening up, getting stuck in the head, and starting to think, "What is this? This is good, that isn't — this is strange," and more of the same. Of course, these attempts to evaluate the situation are only more ways of trying to control it, none of which works.

If you keep it up long enough, then you find yourself thinking, "Oh no! I'm going through the whole song and dance all over again for the ninety-fifth time!" This isn't necessary. Instead of going through it all over again, stop, and begin to assert something progressive within yourself. Start with some composure and some self-control – some heightened sense of awareness to and increased concentration on the moment. These will allow you to distinguish between what is true and creative about it, and what is just excess baggage.

In the practice of meditative techniques, you learn to relax, to be alert, to keep your attention inside, and to go beyond your tendencies to react with fear or resistance. That's what the practice is for. At the same time, to live a spiritual life is not simply a matter of meditating twice a day to become peaceful or composed. Meditation is really for becoming aware of the essence of your own life, and then beginning to live from that essence whether you're walking, riding the subway, working in your job, or doing anything else. True, honest meditation is being aware of that essence at all times. Then whether you're sitting still or moving around is irrelevant. You won't need a specialized environment in order to have the experience. You will have extended the essence of all the techniques into your whole life, and made your life itself an act of meditation.

BY YOUR EFFORT

The potential in your life exists as a range of possibilities. Most people function within only a limited part of their own range, although it doesn't have to be that way. Effort is the linchpin. It is by your determined effort that the natural evolution of what is fully possible will unfold.

AN ORDINARY LIFE

———

The one thing that has always frightened me absolutely is the idea of living an ordinary life. Staying the same for fifty years. That scares me more than anything.

"WORKING THROUGH
PAST STUFF"

———

I heard a term the other day that I hadn't heard in a while. Somebody told me he was "working through some past stuff." I had to chuckle to myself, but I wanted to talk to you about it, because I've noticed that people often feel that there actually is something from the past they have to work through.

Certainly it's true that all of us have many experiences that have represented some big effort on our part at one time or another. In spite of what you may think, however, the effort you need to make now is not one of figuring out these experiences themselves, because that's practically impossible. Rather, the effort must continually be one of reaching inside yourself, opening your heart and mind, and feeling the flow of energy within you. This means allowing those past experiences to be absorbed deeply inside of you – deeply beyond your ego and mind – so that whatever their energy may be, it can simply have its effect and be done.

Most people resist doing this. When that's the case, then what they like to call "working through" something is really no more than chasing their own tail. If you do this too, you'll find that first you get tired of chasing your tail; then you get tired, period. After that, it's all finished, but you still haven't really grown from anything. Do you understand? The past is nothing. The past is dead, finished, and gone. It has no meaning, except for the meaning that you give to it. The degree to which you hang on to it is the degree to which it has some effect on your current reality. Otherwise, it's nothing – even less than nothing.

I'll tell you a personal secret. Some time ago, while reading through spiritual books about other people deeply involved in one spiritual practice or another, I had to face the fact that – unlike all of them – I had not been born on a lotus blossom and discovered floating in the middle of the river. At that point, I could have thought, "Well, there's something terribly wrong with my past, so there must be something wrong with me." After all, I came in the same way everyone else did, and we're all going out together. So, that must make all of us limited beings.

Right? Wrong. In no way does this, or anything else about our past, limit the vitality, the magnificence, and the infinite potential of the creative energy within us. What *does* restrict that vitality is our ability to buy into this nonsense about the past, and to keep on investing in it over fifty years without recognizing that it has no value whatsoever. Understand that there is nothing in your past to be ashamed of, embarrassed about, resentful of, hateful towards, disturbed by, or guilty over.

Even though you may think that you have a difficult life, for the most part, people now have the easiest lives they've had for a long time. Few people get everything they want out of life, despite ad campaigns to the contrary, and no one has experiences that are entirely beautiful all of the time. In fact, almost every experience has some complication and at least two sides to it.

You have to understand that all experience is there only for you to transcend and get over. It's not there for you to figure out, understand, analyze, or work through, but only for you to open your heart to it, take it in, digest it, go beyond it, and grow. Period.

Think back to some moment when you had a strong thought or feeling, and you said to yourself, "This is so important that I'm going to remember it always." A month later, were you still remembering it? I doubt it. An insight into the essence of Life Itself is not something you can remember; it is only something in which you can participate. It's not a past thing to be recalled; it is the eternal present to be lived. It's not complicated; it is profoundly simple. What it requires is that you make the effort to rise above the tensions within yourself, and live from a completely different level. Think about it. In those moments when you have really felt your heart open, how much of the past were you thinking about? Not much.

Only when you learn to surrender the past – to let go of it and forget about it – can you begin to have the mindfulness it takes to deal with the tensions that arise in this moment and the next. If you're always stuck in the fifteen feet of emotional concrete you've let harden in you for the past thirty years, how can you talk about "working through" something? How can you ever rise to the level of dealing with tensions in any real way, when you're still only dealing with your own ego?

After every difficult experience, there is a natural cycle during which you absorb the energy that arises from dealing with a strong force. For example, when you lose someone in your life, a specific sequence takes place. First, the shock sets in; next, the pattern congeals and the shock falls away; then, hopefully, a reorganized organism emerges. It is true that this sequence takes time, but it doesn't take thirty years. At most, in its natural course, it takes three months. It takes even less time than that if you learn to open yourself, feel the flow, absorb the energy, and then go forward.

The next time something rough happens to you, instead of sitting down and trying to figure out why God doesn't love you, or what that person meant when he said such and such, or what you should have said when you meant this and that, or why something didn't happen the way you wanted – instead of carrying on and on about all that, just stop it. Reach inside, open your heart, feel the flow, and begin to attune yourself to the deeper place within you that has only a minimal connection with the energy level of the event that is bothering you. Then, you'll be able to stop dragging around ninety-five thousand years of excess baggage. Instead, you'll be able to be completely present in the moment, full of love, and able to nourish the part of your life that is really growing. You won't be exhausting yourself by struggling with the part of your life that is really dying.

Begin to cultivate within yourself the capacity to absorb and flow in the midst of every difficult energy and powerful force. Once you learn to do this, then nothing can knock you off your center. Instead, everything that happens in your life reinforces your basic composure, nourishes you deeply, and exposes you more and more to the reality of the situation through which you're passing. The point is that it's always much more important to be intensely aware of what's going on in the present than it is to figure out what went on in the past. Think about it.

SURRENDER IS NOT WHAT YOU THINK

———

People resist the idea of surrender because they misunderstand what it means. Usually, they think that it means having to submit to some form of domination, and that it represents the loss of some important aspect of their self-esteem. However, to understand what surrender is, you have to think about it in a different way. Start by asking yourself what you think it really means to grow. I'm not talking just about acquiring some new skill, but about undergoing profound inner change. What does a person tend to run away from, if not this? Think about all the ways people can tell themselves, "Well, I really am growing by going here and going there, and by doing this or that," when the truth of the matter may be that they've done all those things to avoid growing, not to en-gage in it.

If you think about growing – about making an effort to become the best person you can possibly be – and you commit yourself to that, then all you surrender in the long run are those things which get in the way of your being that best person. Ultimately, what it boils down to is that you give up fear, hesitation, and excuses. That's all.

A SUBTLE UNDERSTANDING

———

Who we associate with is one of the critical factors in how we will grow and what the quality of our life will be. Often, we go through life and take our associates and acquaintances at face value. But friendship is important and powerful in our lives; we have to be more discriminating than that about our friends. This makes it important to establish attachments with people who we have looked at and studied, and who we understand to be good people – spiritual people – who, through our contact with them and through what we receive from them, will help to promote our growth as a bigger person.

If we really want to grow, the first thing is to have friends who understand what growing is. The next thing is to learn to trust them. Learning to trust is a big issue for every human being. Therefore, to learn real trust, it's better if you have a relationship with someone who has the capacity for it, and who deserves the trust. This is something you have to work at. You may get burned by it sometimes, but that's all right, because in the process you will also learn about trust. The one thing you can't do is to become cynical because you then cut yourself off from learning anything about trust.

Trust is a subtle understanding; it is a powerful awareness. When you learn to trust another person, two things happen. First, your consciousness expands tremendously. You become a completely mature person, and you learn to trust Life Itself. This is the beginning, if you will, of the unfolding of your relationship with God. Another way of saying it is that it's the beginning of the unfoldment of your understanding of the whole universe. But until you trust Life Itself, you will never find this fulfillment. Think about this, because I've said something vastly general, but still significant.

So much of what we strive for as spiritual people is the strength and understanding simply to trust. It is out of our capacity to trust that real love emerges. Until that trust is established, we may get hot flashes and feel the kind of love you hear about on the AM radio, but that's not the kind of love I'm talking about. That comes and goes. This doesn't.

In Eastern spiritual traditions and, for that matter, in any endeavor to grow, one reason a mentor – a teacher – is important is that the essence of the relationship between a teacher and student is basically one of trust. You make a decision to trust *this*, and from there you learn about trust in a more general way. In the process of learning about it, your capacity for trust expands. Then, slowly, you discover that part of awakening consciousness involves learning that, on the deepest level, you can trust everybody.

THE ROLE OF THE TEACHER

———

The role of the teacher is basically twofold: first, to arouse the deepest creative power of Life present within you; then, to support you as this power unfolds. As this happens, the creative power of Life makes you aware of the intimate interrelationship of all spirit and matter, and of the oneness of all spirit. Supported by the teacher, you enter into an experience of union not only with the teacher, but also with that teacher in whom your own teacher is unified, and with the Teacher from whom all things have come forth.

What starts this in the first place is a simple experience of love between you and the teacher. That's the reality of it. That simple contact, which you cultivate and express in ways that are honest for you, is what allows the energy to grow, and what allows you continuously deeper access to it. This communion with the teacher should expand you, and bring you more and more into a sense of communion with every aspect of your life – even the parts you don't care for very much.

At different points in time, various aspects and experiences will dominate the field of your awareness. Even so, they never separate you from the teacher. For me, there is no day when I don't literally experience the presence of my teachers in the total field of my awareness. For this I am profoundly grateful.

This doesn't mean that you can't be detached from the teacher. Separation and detachment are two different things. Detachment is seeing through the objects of our attachment, and understanding that what we've been attached to wasn't ever really there in the first place. This includes not only the personality but also the physical presence of the teacher.

Furthermore, the physical teacher represents both a support and a resource – not a conspiracy to make you bound and dependent. The physical teacher doesn't exist to dominate your life, and no teacher with half a brain would even want to. What would be the point? Instead, the teacher is simply like a well from which you draw a clear, pure vitality which supports the process of your regeneration and transformation. It may take the form of advice, instruction, or a subtle but powerful exchange of energy; all of these are ways in which this fundamental essence articulates its creative power.

People worry about turning to a teacher. They feel they should do their spiritual work all on their own. They overlook the fact that at no time do you ever work anything out independently or alone, because none of us is ever really independent or alone in any situation. We are always interdependent with many, many things. Our life is really a tapestry, with a myriad of threads working their way through it. The role of the teacher is to promote the broadest possible perspective and the deepest possible understanding of this.

CRYSTALLIZATION

———

The term "crystallization" means "stuck." For example, suppose I have a set attitude about how I want my life to be. I say that I want a family, and that I want it to function as a family unit. Therefore, the children have to do certain things, the wife has to do certain things, I'm going to do certain things and, by God, that's how it's going to be! That is the crystallization of an attitude.

Or, suppose I decide that I hate a certain kind of person. That, too, is a crystallization. Attitudes, beliefs, ideas, and finally, concepts about ourselves and the world, are all crystallizations of energy. For example, anger is such a crystallization. So are desires, expectations, and attachments. Even the body is a crystallization of energy, as is a chair. If you burn the chair, the energy is released. If you burn the expectation, the attachment, or the desire through your inner work, energy is released to a whole different level.

You will know that there is crystallization present in any given moment because you'll feel a great deal of resistance, and all kinds of emotions will be provoked. Your practice is then to work to release the energy stuck in these patterns of crystallization, and to come to an awareness that all you really are is the flow of that energy itself.

TENSION IS THE
CRYSTALLIZATION
OF PRESSURE

———

All pressure is only energy which will offer you either support or resistance. You decide which it will be. When you're under pressure, if you get stuck in yourself and close up inside, then you block the flow of energy within yourself. Instead of flowing with the pressure, absorbing it, and transforming it in a creative way, you get stuck against it. Then it can only push you down. At that point, the pressure crystallizes within you as tension, signalling your resistance to change.

At the same time, all pressure always has the capacity to nourish and promote you endlessly. When you are able to flow within yourself and within your environment, then that flow allows the pressure you experience to support you. It can lift you up, as long as you continue to re-late to it openly. Of course, as it does so, it may crunch a few bones, along with your brain and heart, but it *will* transform you as a person.

Your barometer to all this is your awareness of your energy centers (*chakras*), as well as the degree to which they are open, and to which you feel the flow within you. This flow will always tell you where you are. The more you open to it, the greater your capacity to absorb pressures of every kind.

The final point to this is for you to absorb the pressure your own inner chemistry creates as a reaction to the thought of its own death. After all, from a biological point of view, what is the ultimate pressure, if not death? To hold your concentration through even this is to change your entire view of the world. Then, every other pressure that arises suddenly seems of little importance.

GROWING

———

Growing is the most important and essential endeavor that a human being can undertake. You can make and lose money; you can be promoted and demoted in the world. Never, at any stage, is there any certainty about what will happen to you in this life. However, there is one thing that nobody can ever take away from you – the growth you attain through your own search for Self-knowledge. Furthermore, this growth and understanding become the foundation that sustains you through any and all worldly difficulties, and that allows you – whatever the form of your physical experience – to find in life a continuously unbroken flow of total well-being.

FIVE FINGERS, FIVE FLEAS

The desire to change something about yourself is a little bit like trying to put five fingers on five fleas. Every time you get two or three pinned down, the others crawl off in all directions. Identifying too much with different personality traits that you're not happy about in yourself is just as great a waste of time. Between scratching and reaching to get at them, all you end up with is frustration.

Furthermore, the minute you start thinking that way, you develop a problem-consciousness. In other words, you identify a problem in your personality, and you set out to conquer it. Maybe you even succeed in doing so, and you feel good about that. Then, you turn around and see fifty others you have to deal with, so you take on the next one, and the next, and the next. Finally, you run up against something in your personality that you can't conquer, and you get frustrated.

In the process of doing this, you suddenly discover that all the problems you thought you had already solved are back again. Then, you either decide that you're a terrible person after all, and that it's only a matter of time before everybody finds out – at which point you become totally compulsive about trying to fix yourself – or you get completely discouraged, and give up.

I wouldn't pay too much attention to all that. The thing to pay attention to is the degree of openness and grace, as well as the sense of flow that you have all along within yourself and with other people. Generally, you'll find that people are very forgiving of your eccentricities. As for those who aren't, what are you going to do? You can't live with everybody. All you can do is concern yourself with the big picture in terms of your direction, the quality of your effort, the power of your concentration, and your own consistency. Then, in time, the details of your personality will work themselves out and change in their own way.

YEARNING

Yearning is a part of the beginning of anybody's practice. You have to yearn to grow. You can't want it one day, but not the next, and expect to make any real progress. You have to begin with some steady, inner hunger. The paradox is that at the same time as you cultivate that yearning on the one hand, the experience of the fulfillment of that yearning is also readily available to you in your practice. This means that the beginning stage and the fulfillment stage are both part of every meditation. It starts out one way, finishes up differently, and what you have experienced are the poles of human awareness – the poles of the pulsation of the breath.

FEAR AND PAIN NEVER DISAPPEAR

I don't think that fear or pain ever disappear. I could tell you that they do but, realistically, they're always there somewhere around the fringes. What does happen, however, is that your understanding becomes more powerful. When fear and pain arise again, you then have more strength to deal with them. I would imagine that no matter how many times you look death dead in the eye, your cells and chemicals will still get a tingle out of it. Hopefully, however, your awareness does not waver, and your concentration is not scattered or diminished.

Swami Muktananda used to say that fear doesn't exist – that it's not real, even though you think you experience it. It would be easy enough for me to say this too, but I choose not to for a specific reason. I could tell you, "Oh, there's no such thing as pain. There's only the bliss of the Self" – and, in a way, this is so. Still, however, the experiences of fear and pain are always there.

Suppose I said, "There's no such thing as pain" to people just beginning this practice. They would get started, and sooner or later, run up against some pain. Then they could think only one of two things: either that there was something wrong with them, or that I was a liar. It would be like a dentist telling you that something doesn't hurt. What do you mean, it doesn't hurt? Understand that the Divine has two aspects. These two things – pain and bliss – are always present, and close together. It's the subtle balancing of your own mind in your concentration on the energy of Life Itself, that makes pain and joy one and the same experience.

There are real things to be dealt with here. Real powers. The biological imperatives to eat and to reproduce function continuously as the contracted expression of the creative power of Life Itself. They are extremely powerful. To see beyond the chemistry of your body – to see through the cloud, into the essence of its composition – demands a lot of you. To come to understand that you don't exist in the ways you always thought you did – that there's really no such thing as this body, that there's no such thing as this mind, that these feelings are not real – this, too, is powerful.

To be able to experience this at all first requires that you cultivate the capacity to deal with pain. The only way to do this is to open your heart to it every single day –

to surrender to it. To let it come inside you without resisting it in the slightest but rather, to let it penetrate you as deeply as it wants, and then to work its way through you. This requires a real effort. It requires that you learn to allow all of the tensions, and all of the energy and power of Life Itself to reach deeply into you and change you.

This change hurts. On some days, you'll sit there feeling as though everything is burning away your mind. On other days, you'll feel as though the cosmic dentist is drilling into every one of your *chakras* at once. On one of those days, you'll come to me, and tell me what's happening. Do you want me to say, "Oh no, it's not!" If I do, you'll think that something is wrong with one of us.

The truth is that growing is real work. Being a big person is hard. It's made all the more difficult by the fact that nobody is going to give you a nickel for being a big person. The bigger a person you become, and the stronger you are, the more burdens you will carry. Yet, because of the power of love within you, they're not burdens at all. You learn that it's not the recognition that's essential. Instead, it's the extraordinary joy of participating in, and observing the unfoldment of the most wondrous and amazing power of Life Itself, with its endless vitality, and endless freedom to change. It is from the strength of this understanding that you face your fears and your pain, and deal with them.

"GOOD ENOUGH"

There are areas in each of us that may not correspond to the norms of social perfection. Don't bother about them. Instead of dwelling on your weaknesses – and everybody has them – accentuate the things you do very, very well. Dwell on these things, and everybody around you will be finding ways to excuse you. If, however, you focus on your weaknesses, then everybody else will be kicking you about them too, because you probably won't even be doing the things that you could be doing well. You'll be too busy focusing on your weaknesses.

One of the current movements that I least like is the modern tendency toward hyper-self-analysis. It promotes people's constantly looking at, dwelling on, and wallowing in what they think are their deficiencies. When it comes right down to it, who cares? Maybe at this stage in your life it doesn't make sense for you to try to train for the Miss America contest. Maybe your time and energy are better spent elsewhere. That's fine.

You know, the other day, a friend of mine brought me a *Dr. Strange* comic book. In the back, there was an advertisement that read, "Get into great physical shape. You, too, can go from being a two hundred and fifty pound weakling, to a three hundred and fifty pound strong man." I looked in the mirror, and said, "That's for me" – so I sent in the coupon. They sent back a package, which showed me that for just $1,999.95 and fifteen years, I too could be – "good enough."

THE HEART ILLUMINES
THE MIND

————

It is the experience of what resides deeply in your heart that gives rise to an illuminated mind – a mind filled with wisdom and knowledge, with understanding and compassion. You can think all you want, and get nowhere. It is the heart that illumines the mind, not the other way around.

RED SUNS AND WHITE-WASHED FENCES

————

A few weeks ago, a man came up to me after one of my talks and said something like, "During sex, I felt a tremendous rush of energy, and all the sexual fluid went up my spine to the top of my head. It was incredible. I've been having sex every day after that, trying to recapture the feeling." I looked at him and said that I didn't tend to take that kind of experience too seriously. I haven't seen or heard from him since.

I bring this up with you to illustrate an important point: we often have a tremendous desire to evaluate our own growth — to measure our spiritual accomplishment. "Let's all look for the red sun in meditation — and let's make it really important. If we see it once, maybe — my

God! – maybe that even means something. Then we can spend the rest of our lives trying to see it again!" In the whole religion business, over and over again you'll find this tendency to get everyone looking for something that isn't there, or that means very little even if it *is* there. Do you see the problem inherent in this whole idea? It's an arrangement worthy of Tom Sawyer and I'll bet somebody's ending up with a lot of whitewashed fences.

The point is this. Sometimes you may have powerful visionary experiences; you may see different places, past lives, gods and goddesses, other planets and universes, and any number of other things. You may even have extraordinary physical experiences. But the truth is that they all boil down to the same thing: not one of them will give you so much as a thimbleful of nourishment.

It's easy to sit down, close your eyes, and wait for some angel to come down and kiss you on the forehead. Indeed, this has become many people's idea of spiritual work – "Let's see God!" Such people exhaust their energy running after the fantastic, the amazing, and the supercosmically orgasmic. To put it bluntly, this is crap.

In searching for ways to evaluate your own growth, you may want these extraordinary experiences to mean something, because they let you think that you've gotten somewhere. Then, because you've made them mean something, you want to have them over and over again to validate the effort you're making within yourself. It gets to a point where you feel almost forced to have them over and over again, because without them you'll feel as if you've fallen off some special spiritual wagon.

It is not the ego that grows. But because the ego is so attached to its own existence, it is quite natural for it to take these subtle spiritual manifestations or visionary experiences and build them into the framework of its own self-justification. This is foolishness. Having visions of angels and heavens is about as significant an indicator of growth as is making one hundred and fifty thousand dollars a year, or eighty thousand dollars a year. Even ten dollars a year. None of these means anything in terms of growing. To equate having visionary or powerful physical experiences with having truly grown is a big mistake. It is a flimsy spiritual materialism, which you should rigorously avoid. Otherwise, you set yourself up for a major disappointment – one that will enable you first to perpetuate the ever-popular pattern of self-rejection, and then to decide that your spiritual practice, like other things in your life, simply doesn't work.

So, you might wonder, how are you supposed to notice whether or not something called growth is actually happening? You won't like my answer. You tell whether or not you're growing by two things: first, by the depth of your ability to stay open; and secondly, by the extent of your capacity to serve not only your own inner Self and the creative force of Life within you, but also that of your fellow human beings. You must do the two things at the same time, while in the midst of pressure and tension. A perfect balance between the two is, itself, the demonstration of your understanding, your accomplishment, and your mastery. It is the measure of your growth. It is also the *test* of your growth, which is why we call what we do "work." It is easy to seek something that's not there.

It is a greater challenge to face what *is* here in front of you: to open your heart, to find within yourself and within your own life – just as it is – the extraordinary creative force that is the essence of all abundance and fulfillment, and to sustain your contact with that force. In the end, the real test of your growth is not your having attained different kinds of spiritual experience; rather, it is your ability to serve Life Itself. That is reality.

BROKEN RADIOS AND OCEAN WAVES

You've heard me say this many times: the mind itself is like a broken radio. Its nature is static. This is no obstruction to your practice, however, because quieting the mind is different from stilling the mind.

The mind becomes stilled in the awareness of something much deeper within you. It's like the surface of water. If you plunge into the ocean, the waves continue on the surface. They never stop. Even on the calmest day, there is still a slight ripple. But when you're in the depths of the ocean itself, you don't notice this. You notice only the dynamic stillness of the deep.

MENTAL DISCIPLINE

———

There are two things to understand about mental discipline. The first is the importance of cultivating the general attitude that there are not really two – or even multiple – things in the world, but only one thing. If there's only one thing, and that one thing is the very essence of all Life, then wherever you look, however you speak, and whatever you do through your life, is something you express from your Self to your Self. Understanding this should have the effect of causing you to be a lot more respectful and careful about how you look at and talk to the world. It doesn't mean that you can't make jokes, but it does imply something about the spirit in which you should express yourself.

The second thing is that, from this attitude of oneness – this holistic perception that there is fundamentally no separation between yourself and anything else – you should also try to understand nonattachment. The various tensions you experience – the guilt, the fear, the ambition, and the greed – are really your attachments to your different attitudes, apprehensions, and desires. A different way to put this would be to say that tensions are your attachment to a basic misunderstanding of how things are. Nonattachment is therefore actually an extension of a holistic attitude because if there's only one thing, then what is there to be attached to?

Understanding that there's no justification at all for any of these attachments, slowly you cultivate within yourself a state of complete inner peace. This is the state in which you can begin to explore the vitality of your innermost Self – which is also the inner Self of everything. Then, there is no need for attachment to anything.

After a while, living with a holistic attitude and with nonattachment brings your mind into a state of total, dynamic stillness. It is then that the panorama and the vitality of the inner Self are displayed to you as the form of the whole universe. This can come only from a mental discipline that overrides all your conditioning to think, relate, and behave according to an entirely different track.

Think carefully about how a person with a holistic attitude might express himself or herself toward others, and toward the various difficulties that he or she encounters in life. Think about it deeply, so that as the different circumstances that confront you arise, you have already done some preparation. This is the essential mental discipline.

Recognizing that there's really only one thing compels you to think and act in a manner that promotes everybody's best interest at the same time. At the very least, it compels you to try to find that point where everybody's interests *can* be promoted. With a holistic attitude and living with nonattachment, you create around yourself a spacious environment in which everything beneficial to you and to other people can grow. There, the vitality, the power, and the grandeur of the inner Self are continuously revealed, showing it for what it is.

This is not due to your beneficence or to my benevolence. It is not caused by the ideas, the understanding, or the conditions of any person or group. It is simply the purity of the energy itself which is unfolded – and it's dazzling.

BREAKING CYCLES

————

One of the purposes of any spiritual discipline is to break the big cycle. It's talked about in some instances as breaking the cycle of death and rebirth. The point is this: first you add some discipline to your life; then that discipline, and the way you stick to it, becomes the barometer of how you're dealing with past patterns. Through your discipline and effort, you take the energy that you ordinarily allow to flow into a particular pattern, and change its direction. In this way, you change the whole pattern of your life.

At some point, you come to one of those issues where you've gotten stuck before. Since you've been there already, you also know what it looks like when you're on your way to it. However, maybe this time you decide that it's too tiring to go there once again, and that you're willing to make the effort it takes to go someplace different.

This takes a serious commitment. Not a *heavy* commitment, but a real determination. The degree to which it's possible for a person to change is extraordinary, if you really pay attention to it. It all has to do with your willingness to control your own energy. Nor does this commitment require doing a lot of big things. Instead, it's the simple things that, together, are the most effective – the little moments in between, when you're slowly building a different pattern. Like anything that you practice, if you try to be simple and regular about this every day, then you take the steam out of the big moments – the blow-up points. This is the way to begin to break the cycles in your life.

THE LONELINESS LOOP

———

Basically, I see loneliness as an illusion. If you take your meditation practice to a level where, instead of just sitting down and breathing, you begin to feel moving through you the flow of Life and the creative energy which you are, then from your practice itself, you experience a nourishment, a satisfaction, and a joy that transcend your physical existence. At that point, how can anyone talk about loneliness?

Look at the extreme alternative. This involves absorbing yourself in thinking about how lonely you feel. You may try meditating a little bit, but give up on it when it doesn't yield quick results. Still feeling lonely, you then think, "Really what I need is – I guess I need a soulmate!" At that point, you go off on a quest for a soulmate, and run through eighteen or twenty relationships. Each time, you think, "This is it!" but then, six weeks into the thing, you're forced to recognize, "Oh no, it's not." Doing this over and over again to the point of exhaustion, you finally give up the notion of finding a soulmate, saying, "Oh, this spiritual stuff is all crap, anyway."

At that point, you just settle for somebody who's willing to live with you. By then, you're so disgusted that you go out and get a job you didn't want in the first place, persuade yourself that you're happy at it, and then go home, eat dinner, watch television, and forget about it. Clearly, I've exaggerated, but you get the point.

All of this means that you have to be careful. You have to think it through before you let yourself get absorbed in feelings such as loneliness. If you indulge in them, in the long run they overpower you. Never will they take you where you wanted to go, or even where you thought you were going. Instead, all they do is convert your energy into tension, in a self-reinforcing feedback loop. Your task is to remember that you don't have to get caught up in it in the first place.

WHEN TO DECLINE

Generally speaking, when you're not ready to do something you'll have a genuine sense on the front side of your inability to fulfill the task. You may still take on the responsibility, hoping unreasonably that you can carry it out, but these are actually the sorts of tasks you should decline. This sincere sense of being unable to do something is different from resistance. Resistance to a task more often sounds something like "I don't really want to do this!" In fact, most of the time, it's a case of "I don't want to," and not "I really can't."

If you're certain that you'll let somebody down, then you decline the responsibility. But if there's some question, then you have to think about it a little bit more. For one thing, what does the particular responsibility have to do with the overall flow of your life? You have to ask yourself, "Am I just resisting, or is this something I have good reason to turn down?"

There's no need to take on any responsibility thoughtlessly – especially one that involves other people's lives. So after giving it some careful thought, you make the best decision you can. You'll never find a program for doing this, because too many things always feed into any given decision for there to be any rules. Some decisions will end up being objective and rational, while others will be purely intuitive.

People most resist taking on more responsibility and deepening their involvement in creative projects. They resist that deeper responsibility for one simple reason – it cuts into their fool-around time. However, this is totally different from not being ready to take on the task. To be honest with yourself is to recognize the difference quite clearly.

TO TURN THE ANGER INSIDE

One thing you can do when you start to feel anger welling up is to notice where in your body you feel it. You might find that your stomach starts to knot up just below the navel, or that your chest starts to tighten, or that your throat gets dry. (Generally, your throat gets tight when you get emotional, and not angry, but the two can go together.) These tight places are *chakras* that have become contracted.

Take your attention into the places where you feel tightness and, one by one, start to relax them. If you can sense the energy within your anger, and if you can concentrate on feeling *that* flowing down the front of your body like a current, and then up your spinal column, it means that you are taking the energy that is the real force within the anger, and redirecting it in a progressive way. Instead of expressing it outside yourself, you are turning it inside.

This idea sometimes confuses people. They think that to turn anger inside means to repress it and to end up with an ulcer. This is not what I mean. To turn anger – or any other strong emotion – inside in this way is not to suppress it, but to recover the basic energy that it is. You reclaim that energy, and use it to uplift you.

The second thing to do, if you can't do that, is to drop your hands to your sides, hold your fingers out a little bit, and feel the anger draining out the ends of your fingers. If you try this, you will feel a real sensation that goes from the center of your chest, up, out, and down the arms. This is a simple practice, and is actually much more than just a technique for dealing with anger. Like the first technique, this is part of the larger system of *kundalini yoga*, and anger is only one facet of everything that it addresses. In a general way, you could say that this particular case is an example of the way in which *kundalini yoga* works to conserve your more dynamic and creative energy from the contractions and contortions in which it can get tied up.

FEAR ACTS LIKE A CENTRIPETAL FORCE

———

Fear is something that arises for most people. The reason for this is that any time a new area opens up for us, we recognize that allowing ourselves to flow into it will change us completely – and every human being has an innate and natural resistance to change. We know what we are already, but we don't know what we might become – or what might become of us.

Fear lies at the very foundation of what I call the *mantra* of stupidity – "What's going to happen to me?" If you think like this, all you do is wrap nets around yourself. This is because fear is a contraction of your energy. Into the space created because of that contraction, every kind of illusion arises. This is a self-feeding mechanism that only strengthens the ego. At the same time, it is a dualistic experience, because it reinforces your sense that you are separate from everything else and need to protect yourself. This dualism is the fundamental cause of pain and suffering.

You have to override it. You have to make a conscious, determined effort within yourself to change the program. This is actually quite simple. What you have to do is to want deeply to grow. To want to grow in this way connects you to what is possible in your life. This is of complete benefit to you as an individual.

Otherwise, fear acts like a centripetal force, drawing you back into the same patterns for which you have been programmed by much of your upbringing and experience. It draws you into the same orbit – the same original sin, if you will. Instead, feel deeply within yourself, and require of yourself that you grow as a person.

YOU ARE NOT IN THIS LIFE
TO HAVE THINGS GO
YOUR WAY

———

You are not in this life to have things go your way. It's utterly and totally unreasonable to expect that they will. What you do have are a number of diverse resources within yourself and within your environment, as well as a deep, simple, creative awareness. The real challenge of this life is not to find the perfect situation, because there is no such thing. Nor is it to get your own way. Rather, it is to connect with your own inner resources and with the opportunities that exist in the atmosphere. Then, through the understanding that you cultivate within yourself, you merge the two and make a creative expression that, at its core and in its essence, is perfection.

MAKING THE WHOLE
THING FIT

─────

My response, during challenging events, is to be quiet in the moment, and not to react or talk too much. Responding to any challenge quickly is not likely to result in anything thoughtful. The best thing is to be as quiet as possible, and to think about the matter for a while before expressing your reaction. Even if somebody says, "I want to know right this second," you don't have to give an answer. You can say, "Well, I don't know right this second, but I'll tell you tomorrow." You never have to answer in the moment.

There is also another level to this discussion. The real challenges in your life are not the ones that come right in a moment, in a flash, bringing a lot of dust and heat with them. For example, the real challenge is not when somebody comes up to you and says, "Your mother wears combat boots." Many times, people come up to me and say, "I don't like that orange dress of yours." I suppose I could go into a long explanation about what kind of clothes swamis are expected to wear, but why get into it? I just say, "Neither do I, but I can't afford another one."

The point is, these are not the challenges. The real challenges are the ones that take time to face. They challenge your limited understanding, your limited capacity, and the ways in which your emotions and your mind inhibit the flow of your creative energy.

The whole pattern is the challenge – not the little things. Suppose you're a musician, and you pick a complicated piece of music to perform. The real challenge lies not just in the hard parts of the piece, but in bringing all the parts together, and in making the performance greater than the sum of all the individual notes. Isn't that so? Furthermore, masterful technique alone does not add up to masterful presentation. The challenge is much bigger than mastering various complicated sets of notes. It involves making the whole thing fit.

To get entangled in various superficial, technical issues steals your energy and depletes your capacity to rise to the real occasion. Don't allow yourself to get sucked into superficial issues. Keep your mind focused on the big ones, and don't bother so much about the little ones. Forget the petty things that ordinarily occur in your day and that attempt to sidetrack your concentration and your mind from the important issues.

Let me give you a different example: a businessman has an overall business plan that he wants to follow. He has objectives and goals for his group that he wants to see put into action. He sets out every day to implement these goals and everything that the group has discussed. In the course of doing this, he gets ninety-seven phone calls about one thing or another, his dog gets chased around the block by a cat and is now missing, and his landlady calls him to tell him that the kitchen's flooded. Suddenly, his concentration is gone.

It's always the case that anything can steal your attention away from implementing the creative work you've been trying to develop – if you let it. At the same time, if you do start to react to something, you can always reset your focus on what you're trying to accomplish, and remind yourself of what you're really about. If you read the *Vijñanabhairava*, there are over a hundred individual techniques for refocusing your attention on what's important. Pick any one of them – most of them you can even do while riding on the subway. For one thing, you can breathe. Sometimes, that's the challenge. The point is to remember that you always have a choice in how you respond to any situation.

A DYNAMIC STILL POINT

Meditation is about changing patterns within yourself
by bringing your mind to a still point over and over again.
Each time, you concentrate within yourself; each time,
you connect deeply within yourself. Your whole field of
attention contracts to a dynamic still point, within
which is released whatever pattern of restriction is functioning at that moment. What replaces it is a broader,
finer pattern. Over time, this event frees you from the
limitations of your physical body, of your mind, and of
your emotions. It's true that this is work – but it's a
joyous work.

A REAL TEACHER

———

I've been fortunate in many ways, but one of the most fortunate things in my life has been that when I met my teacher, it took me all of two and a half seconds to know it. I simply knew that this was my teacher, and that I was there to work and to learn. Two and a half seconds, and not a moment of doubt. Is it necessary to know this? I think that it's important (even if it takes you a little longer than two and a half seconds!) At the same time, it can present a dilemma, because there are so many teachers, and so many of them are spiritual Coney Islands. (It's possible that I'm Coney Island too, but I work hard not to be.)

The one thing I can tell you, which might help, is this: a real teacher will always turn the energy back on you, and will always turn you back to yourself. Your work with a real teacher will never be a case of the student worshipping the teacher. A real teacher will demand of you that you be both grounded in this world and reaching to uplift yourself. The focus will always be on *you*. A teacher may ask you to help to support the community in some way, but, if you don't have money, that will never be a problem. Nor will there ever be a belief system involved, because you go to a real teacher to learn to believe in yourself, and not in some set of rules. When you believe in yourself, and touch the potential within yourself – even for a moment – then you'll know where God is. There will be nothing to discuss. You'll just know.

OF BEGINNINGS

Some people can't understand why they find it so difficult to begin spiritual work on a regular basis. They get up in the morning, and the first things they think about are the tasks ahead of them for the day. They go out to do them, and they meet with all the contracted energies and every other complexity that could obstruct their efforts. Indeed, this is the way the world teaches people to conduct their lives. Only after all *that* are they to think about their spiritual practice, as something to tack on when all the "important" things have been taken care of. Not surprisingly, by that point a person feels, "Oh, I'm too tired already!" and gives up on the idea of developing a spiritual practice.

If, on the other hand, you start out each day with your inner work, and as you move through the day, try to meet each opportunity that presents itself from your own center, then you establish a sense of joy, vitality, and enthusiasm for life. You engage this joy – you dance with it, if you will. Then, whatever the activity, it's not even quite an issue of work any more; it's an act of love. You find that you're tireless in it. You have all the energy you require for anything.

It's a question of where you begin, and of what you understand your real work to be. Try to start out with an intense love of life, and an intense love of God. Then, go wherever that love takes you, and do whatever you're called upon to do from there.

PASSING BY THE BANQUET

——

The one good point to being a human being is your intimate and infinite interconnectedness with the Divine. This is so not just because I'm telling you about it; it's so because you yourself know it. You've felt it within yourself on many occasions. When I came out of a Catholic background in the Midwest to seek a fine *guru* and to pursue all this, it was because I felt there was something deeply special within me. I was willing to do whatever it took to find it, and to live in it and from it. It's because this same thing is within each of us, calling out to us, that anybody pursues anything like a spiritual life.

It is by the grace of God that such an idea dawns on our minds in the first place. It just takes a little courage to let go of the tensions of this world, and of all the struggle, conflict, frustration, and disappointment that it presents. It takes a little courage to begin to live from within, and to live up to that inner specialness.

The world will always offer you a banquet of rabbit pellets, cow pies, bull puckeys, and road apples. This is what the world feeds everyone. Some people even like it a lot. They gather up great quantities, and gobble them down. I'd say, forget it. A person can always skip dinner a few times, and find out whether the hunger that follows as a result may not actually be the yearning to learn something about living from within.

DEALING WITH TENSIONS IS NEVER WHAT IT SEEMS

———

Infinite volumes of spiritual literature can be reduced to the simple choice a person has in life: either to be consumed by tensions or to rise above them. It's that simple. The tensions by which we become consumed, and with which we identify, are bondage. They lead us to live a reactionary existence, and represent the ability to immerse ourselves in a completely short-term perspective.

The alternative is to open ourselves to tensions, absorb them as energy, be transformed by that conscious effort, and live from an increasingly universal and progressive perspective. Instead of feeding the tensions and having the polarity between ourselves and others endlessly increase, we can dissolve the polarity and dissolve the ego, thereby recognizing and living in a state of complete unity and harmony with Life Itself.

We have the opportunity to choose many times every day: we can make an effort to be open, and to live with a genuine love and respect for ourselves and for others; we can choose to speak and act carefully, and with consideration; we can choose to see all our inner effort not only as an exploration of the extraordinary potentiality of the conscious energy within ourselves, but also as an outer investment in the quality of our life. We can choose all this or we can let ourselves be consumed by doubts, fears, worries, and insecurities.

We choose, and every day we act out our choice. The depth of our commitment to our spiritual process shows itself in many ways. We demonstrate the reality of our own motivations through our interactions with, and through the quality of, the environment we create. It's important to understand this so that we can look at ourselves in a realistic way, and begin to make our choice a conscious one. We decide which it will be.

In addition to not always recognizing the degree to which they have a choice in dealing with tensions, there is one thing people often misunderstand. It's like this. If you ever have a chance to look out on the ocean at sunrise or sunset, notice how the sun seems to break over the horizon really quickly, and to drop down just as fast. Actually, however, by the time you see a sunrise or sunset, it's already happened several minutes before. You just don't see it that way because of how light travels and how your senses work.

This means that before you judge any difficulty to be a bad thing, you have to be a little bit thoughtful. For instance, the whole process of healing begins with the elimination of a lot of poison from the system. As this happens, the whole system feels pretty sick.

This, itself, is part of the healing process. It's not a symptom that something has gone wrong; it's a symptom that something is going right. If you have an injury and you feel no pain whatsoever, what does that tell you? The injury killed you! The experience of pain can therefore actually signify the initiation of the healing process.

Yet many times when we feel pain, we identify it in a certain way, and thereby reinforce the stress involved in the whole experience. The inability to understand that our senses often deceive us can lead us to make judgments about pain that are inappropriate to the real nature of our inner condition. Subsequently, we react in ways that are inappropriate to promoting health in our physical system, health in the mental and emotional systems, and certainly, fulfillment in our spiritual life. In other words, instead of facilitating healing, our own attitude actually impedes it. This makes dealing with tensions both a craft and an art, as well as a fundamental part of all spiritual development.

So we can see that dealing with tensions is never what it seems. For example, our spiritual work chips away at the solid mass of our inner garbage and loosens a certain amount of it. When all that garbage surfaces, usually people want to dive into it and swim around. Instead, what we have to do is be quiet, and let the change move through our system and get out of there already. As we become aware of the garbage itself (possibly for the first time), we may feel various degrees of self-loathing. We may think we're experiencing a big struggle, and we may judge it to be a bad thing. To me, however, it looks like a good thing, and not like something we should fight.

Instead of relating to what's on the horizon, or to what we're feeling and sensing about ourselves – and in every way allowing these things to color our interactions with life – look underneath all that, and focus on an inner purity. In the beginning, the purity may be in our intention to improve ourselves and to grow as a person. In the end, it becomes a purity of love that is the essence of total well-being. Then, instead of identifying with difficulty, we put it behind us – which is where all difficulty really exists.

Because of the investment we make every day in this understanding, over time we dissolve all past and future tensions. To dissolve all past and future tensions means that we live in a timeless state – one in which we're able to be still, and know within ourselves the infinite nature of the Divine and of our own inner Self.

We not only dissolve these tensions; we also let go of them. This is the true renunciation – not denying or rejecting tension, but merely not holding on to it any longer. This renunciation leads to a complete transcendence. Transcendence doesn't mean that we go from one place to another, but rather that by the power of our concentration and ability to sustain the inner flow, we penetrate all the veils. Then we see everything that is and everything that happens as a manifestation of the infinite, conscious, creative energy which flows in us, and in which we flow.

In the process of dissolving these tensions, and as our own creative capacity grows, we also begin to understand that it is essential for us to be desireless. Why? Because basically, all tension arises from desire. As we begin to appreciate the well-being that exists inside the flow, we also begin to appreciate its extraordinary creative power. As we begin to feel this and to live from it, we come to trust it more and more. We begin to see that desire obstructs our capacity to sense and appreciate the full range of creative power implicit in this energy. Then, we simply let go of the desires.

When we let go of desire, we cease to be driven by wanting our life to turn out in particular ways. Then, we can begin to appreciate what our life really is. Instead of endlessly projecting our own limited vision and understanding in the form of our limited desires, we are free to feel, sense, touch and be touched by something much bigger than is easy to imagine or talk about. Every day of our life we can begin to sense this flow and see its effect. We can sense its action and participate in it. We can understand it working in us, and see it working through us into the lives of the people whose lives we touch.

This makes our experience of life deeply satisfying because every day becomes an extraordinary adventure and a continuous revelation. We never really know where it's going to come from, and so a beautiful renewal takes place within us continuously. Because we have no desires, nothing threatens us; because there's no threat, we're free to appreciate everything that happens, in its proper context. Only when we're free from desire can our creative energy find its fullest expression, and reach its highest potential. Only when we don't want anything for it, or from it, is it free to open and reveal itself fully.

This reminds me of a story. One day, Saint Paul was walking down the beach, trying to figure out the Trinity. He was thinking really hard, "Three in one . . . how can that be?" He puzzled and puzzled, but he just couldn't work out a rational solution to the problem. Anyway, he came across a boy on the beach. The boy had dug a hole in the sand, and was trying to pour the ocean into the hole with a toy bucket.

Of course, you know what happens when you pour a bucket of water in a hole in the beach. Saint Paul said, "Hey kid, you can't do that." The boy looked into the bottom of the hole, which was a deep one, and watched the ocean begin to seep its own way in. He turned to Saint Paul and said, "Listen, I'll put the ocean in this hole before you'll figure out the Trinity!"

This says something about the nature of the mind, and about our attempts to use it as a way to grasp at truth. It's impossible. Truth is not something to think out or to intellectualize; it's something to tune into and to feel – and feel and feel and feel – until we really feel it flowing. In fact, whenever we feel our energy coagulating in our head, it means that we're not doing something right. At that moment, we need to take a breath, relax for a moment, and feel what the energy in our head does.

Have you heard the expression, "Some days, you eat the bears, and some days the bears eat you"? It's an expression from Indiana, so maybe you've never heard it. It means, simply, that some days your tensions get you, and some days you get them. The fact of the matter is, you choose. Instead of being consumed by tensions, you have to learn to open within yourself, to feel the flow, to consume all the tension, and to grow to become a big person. If you do it deeply enough and long enough, then you become free – free of all the biological, psychological, and emotional restrictions that endlessly limit human beings to an unfortunately stupid and brutal existence.

Every day, you get to choose who will eat whom. If you've never tasted bear, think of it as broccoli. "It all tastes like broccoli." You've never heard that either? Then I'll tell you another sort of story. My father was a pharmacist in the countryside, where there are still a lot of people who bring things to trade that they've hunted, grown, or raised. Often, people would bring squirrels or rabbits, or possums or turtles. If somebody asked, "So, what does squirrel taste like?"

"Oh, that tastes like chicken."

"And rabbit? What does rabbit taste like?"

"Well, it tastes like chicken, too."

"How about possum?"

"Chicken."

"Turtle?"

"Guess."

So – at least if you live in a vegetarian *ashram* – you could say that it all tastes like broccoli. The point of all this is that we choose, each day, either to be consumed by our tensions, or to consume and transcend them. It's that difficult, and that simple.

CHANGING THE TIRE

———

Personally, I think that to ask "why" something has happened is a stupid question. "How" may be all right, but "why" is stupid. It's stupid because most of the time when you ask *why* something happened to *you*, you'll never really get an answer. More to the point, even if there were an answer and even if you could get it, it wouldn't help you in your spiritual work. People used to ask the Buddha why there was suffering, and he always responded that this question was not conducive to the process of enlightenment. The point in spiritual work is not to remain stuck in thinking about suffering itself, but to go beyond it. When people ask "why," they usually think they're trying to understand something, but more often they're only exhausting themselves by dancing around in their minds with everybody who ever broke their heart.

You live from this moment now into the future. The past is finished, and you don't have to take it with you. Suppose you're driving along and you get a flat tire. You inspect it, but you can't find a nail or a hole. There's nothing. You don't know what happened – the tire's just flat. What do you do? Do you spend a lot of time trying to figure out why exactly this happened to you at this particular time, or do you get out the spare and put it on?

Move on. Most blocks that you associate with the past are simply undigested pieces of experience and undigested energy for you to absorb and go beyond. Asking "why" doesn't allow you to do this. It only keeps you sitting by the side of the road, staring all day at a flat tire.

WHATEVER DANCE,
WHATEVER GAME

————

If you will turn your attention inside yourself every day –
if you will open your mind and heart to feel the flow of
energy within you and to feel your awareness of it expand – then the issues in your life become no issue at all.
Your notion of who is living your life and of who is
motivating your body totally changes. Furthermore, your
understanding and experience of the universal, creative
power of Life in its highest sense brings you complete
peace within yourself. It brings you a total acceptance of
your life within the larger scheme of Life Itself, and a real
appreciation for the opportunities you have to interact
and communicate with this power in any form. Then,
whatever dance you do, whatever game you play, becomes merely the arena in which you discover and express your interchange with this creative flow.

PYRRHIC VICTORIES

By and large, I don't think you have to take control of anything. After the energy of a situation shows you what it wants to do, then you make your decision whether to participate in it or not. Having made that decision, you become responsible for it and you stick to it.

This is different from controlling the situation. Generally speaking, control of any kind involves you in a losing effort, because the struggle for control is essentially egotistical: "I want things to turn out my way, and somehow I'm going to make that happen." This can become a way of life, but usually the people who engage in it end up defeating themselves. Many a Pyrrhic victory has taken place in this kind of struggle – you win, but at the cost of incalculable losses. So you get control, but then what do you have? You can control the form and destroy the substance of almost anything.

This is because, in the last analysis, the creative energy of Life is infinitely powerful, and human beings are not very big on their own. When they try to control this creative energy instead of feeling it and responding to its flow, they get tangled up and lost in what they've taken on. It's really quite arrogant, when you think about it, to talk about controlling either your own life, or anybody else's.

Yet when you learn to connect to that energy and flow in it, slowly your opportunities for self-expression expand and improve. Then you don't need to control anything. The surrender of all efforts to exercise control over the people, places, and things in your life brings about two benefits. One is that it gives you the opportunity to discover yourself. The other is that instead of your having to struggle with your life, Life Itself will lift you up.

PEOPLE WHO WANT THINGS

People who want things usually, in the process of wanting them, chase them away. When you desire a thing, your focus on it is like the nose of a boat, always pushing away the water just in front of it. As you identify things and want them, the energy around your reaching for the thing pushes it away.

It's like reaching for a feather. If you reach for a feather, the energy of your movement through the air pushes it away. The real way to have anything is to want nothing – and then see what comes to you. If you're willing to take whatever comes, and to care for it and cultivate it, then everything comes.

The whole world pursues love, finally. Have love within yourself, cultivate that, and the whole world comes to your door. But if you want love, and you go looking and looking for it, then it's like the story about the man in the desert who wandered around for years, dying of thirst. Every now and then, he would stop, take off his pack, open it up, pull out a thermos bottle, take a drink of water, close it back up again, and keep going.

This is like not being able to find love because it's in the thermos bottle in your backpack. You don't need to go looking for it; it's always there with you already.

WHISTLING A HAPPY TUNE

——

There's a song from *The King and I* that goes, "Whenever I feel afraid, I hold my head up high, and whistle a happy tune, and no one ever knows I'm afraid." I think that this is not a bad antidote for fear, or for any other kind of congested thinking. Thinking and bodily sensations – along with the mind and the body – are all part of one system. If you want to change the system, then you have to change its chemistry, or its vibration. The simplest way to do this is to be happy (or at least to feel some happiness), even if you have to invent a silly reason for it, or to fake it. Instead of allowing some heaviness to circle around in your head, redirect your attention and change the vibration – the tune – within yourself. In this way, you change the feeling.

100

Let me give you an example. The other day, I was walking down the street with one of our dogs. This dog is rather big, which causes some people to feel concern. (The dog, of course, isn't really interested in people; he's more interested in fenceposts and fireplugs.) As we were going down the street, another person approached us.

When she got near us, she saw the dog, and suddenly tensed up. It so happened that the wind was coming in such a direction that the dog didn't catch her scent until she had passed us. At that moment, however, he immediately wheeled around to look at her, because a person who freezes like that goes through a rapid and subtle change in her scent, which attracts the dog's attention. In other words, that person was announcing, "Here's lunch!"

In powerful ways, based on the particular feeling that you have and the scent that you put out, you attract all of your experiences. Therefore, you want to put out a scent – a feeling – that will attract things of a genuinely finer order than your ordinary experience. You do that simply by being happy.

Some people, of course, feel that to do this is like living in a fantasy. They might accuse me of living in a fantasy-land, myself. Well, I suppose that I'm the strangest person I know (except for everybody else I've ever met), and that the *ashram* (our community) is the biggest group of screwballs I've ever encountered – except for everybody I've run into everywhere else. My point is that everything going on here and elsewhere in the world is a fantasy of some kind. In any case, we ourselves create the distinctions between fantasy and non-fantasy.

Some people also worry that choosing to be happy will prevent them from engaging fully in their professional lives. It is true that when you decide to be happy and to make an effort to be in that state, you are definitely generating an inner change. Yet, to do so in no way impinges upon your professional capability or sense of responsibility. In fact, it should enhance every level of your professional functioning, because the degree to which you are more in touch with the pure potential within yourself is the degree to which you are genuinely able to serve other people and other issues. Likewise, the extent to which you remain tangled up and struggling in your own issues is the extent to which your creative energy strangles in a self-destructive process.

Try, instead, to feel into your heart – you can whistle a tune if you want – and feel around for a reason to sense something slightly sweet in there. Breathe into that sweetness, and continue to feel it circulate and expand until a real joy emerges. Breathe into that joy, and start to allow a simple love of life to emerge within you. Then, feel that, letting it flow inside you and around you.

Doing this will resolve every one of your issues because you are no longer on the same level where getting stuck can even happen. Furthermore, when you really feel that fullness, there's no longer any issue of anything being missing, or of anything being there that shouldn't be; everything is simply all right. When you feel that fullness, you are in touch with yourself, and completely responsible. Having dissolved the barriers to being happy, you become able to have a simple, pure, and complete interchange with everything and everyone in your environment.

WHAT IS ALIVE ABOUT YOU IS ALWAYS ALIVE

———

When you understand that what is alive about you remains alive always, then what can you ever worry about again? What can you be afraid of? What can you lose? At the most basic level, this understanding brings a person freedom from fear; at the highest level, it brings a person complete fulfillment. In the middle, it leads you to make a careful effort to concentrate and to develop discrimination.

Understanding that what is alive within you is alive forever, and that what is not alive never was, you no longer require any answers.

TO THE DEGREE THAT YOU WANT TO GROW

We all appear in this world as different patterns of energy, arising from a larger energy field. Another way to put it would be to say that we are each one vibration of energy among many vibrations of that same energy. Each of these vibrations, operating at different frequencies, gives the impression of having a separate existence and a distinct appearance. This leads us to take the apparent differences seriously, and to imagine that everything truly *is* distinct and separate.

The energy patterns that emerge from within us – that we are – along with the ones that arise around us from our participation in the larger energy field, not only give rise to this appearance of separateness in the first place, but also tend to reinforce it. When we encounter other vibrations of the energy, then we think that we're experiencing friction with the people and situations in our lives – we don't usually think of it as energy meeting itself in a different form. Instead, we're convinced that real limits and real boundaries not only exist, but that they need protecting.

So, the issue of limitation arises. Then we get really fancy, and come up with the notion that because we have these limits, we also have problems. We struggle with these problems. We think about them, analyze them, and psychoanalyze them. Yet, oddly enough, the more we struggle with the things about our existence and appearance that differ from those of others (or from what we imagine those of others to be), the more powerful these differences, distinctions, and limits seem to become.

Because of the way we nurture, nourish, cultivate, reinforce, and develop these limits, we suffer more and more. And why not? They're what we've been cultivating, so why shouldn't they become stronger? Clearly, this doesn't work. Clearly, the whole thrust to analyze and intellectualize the unique aspects of the appearance-part of what we are is not in any way going to satisfy the long-term need that we have to get beyond these appearances.

The solution is to begin to pull our attention away from all the analysis and intellectualization of these distinctions – to begin to withdraw our attention into the very source of this appearance and to cultivate our awareness of its essence. Instead of intellectualizing about this source or this essence, we cultivate our understanding and our living contact with it, which gives rise to an expansion within that field of energy and vitality. This we call growth.

It is growing that lifts us up out of the realm of appearance and limitation. It takes our attention and our energy away from these limits, and away from these boundaries. We literally pull energy away from the boundaries and put it in motion as a kind of evolutionary force. This slowly but surely dissolves the limits, as we transcend our understanding of the apparition that we, and all things, are. Our understanding of the essential nature of our life begins to expand and unfold. We being to live in the powerful certainty of the nature of the inner Self, which is, itself, completely uncertain. So, I am suggesting to you that growing is really the answer to the problem of pain, suffering, and disappointment.

The point I want to make is that we grow to the degree we want to grow. That's simple enough. But wanting to grow is not just something that can waft casually through our minds once a week, or once a day when we come to meditation. It must become an ongoing, living reality. In the Bible, it says, "Ask and you shall receive." I don't think they were joking. It is the depth from which we want this growth that makes it begin to take place.

Think of a tree, or of any living event that emerges from within itself. It is the degree to which it obeys its inner commitment to unfold a certain pattern that enables it to overcome all of the resistance and the obstacles in the environment, and to demonstrate itself as a vast and vital manifestation of the energy of Life. In the same way, the extent to which we are connected with that living, inner force is the extent to which we really change and grow spiritually.

The essential idea here is that we grow to the degree we want to grow. We grow to the degree that we mobilize resources that we may not even know we have at the moment. But because we deeply want to grow, because we have this deep passion for knowing God, because we have this deep love of life and love for God, then that love itself becomes a living event within us. It demonstrates every kind of potential to overcome obstacles, to overcome barriers, to move mountains. It certainly allows us to discover within ourselves vast, unrecognized treasures. The stories of many great saints in India as well as the whole of the *bhakti* tradition of great devotion, are based on this understanding of the deep, deep desire to know God – a desire we have to cultivate. In cultivating it, countless extraordinary capabilities organize themselves within us, and manifest for the purpose of our liberation and fulfillment.

This deep desire should, in a way, make a person into something of a fanatic. Not, however, a closed-minded fanatic. Not a fanatic full of judgments about others. This desire should make us fanatics only in the sense that we dedicate ourselves totally to attaining the deepest understanding possible to a human being, and to being relaxed and open in the process of doing so.

At times, we will be almost on fire with the awareness of our desire for growth and the intensity of this process of loving God and being loved by God. In a way, it burns and consumes us. That's a good thing. Then, there are other times when we are deeply relaxed and at peace within ourselves.

In time, there emerges a kind of dynamic tension between the two, which, at first, happens in cycles. For a while, we are very much on fire; then, for a while, we are very much not. As we grow, the two cycles gradually converge and become one, so that we are completely relaxed, at peace, and flowing within ourselves within the world. At the same time, we are completely on fire with the awareness of the Divine, and completely on fire with the participation in love, which is the essence of Life Itself.

What does this have to do with problems? Thinking about problems doesn't solve them. Getting above them, ninety-nine percent of the time, allows them simply to evaporate − or at least, for us to dispatch them with the simplest of effort. What remains in front of us may be only a small amount of what we had thought of as our problems; it also may represent the largest amount of work we have to do. Real work. But at least we have burned off the fog, and gotten rid of all the illusory programs that were causing us to chase our tail. Then we can begin to deal in a simple and direct way with the real work that we have to do in this life, in order to give expression to the potential that exists within us for our own fulfillment.

I want to reinforce that I am not saying we should simply ignore the various difficulties we encounter in our environment. I'm not saying that we should ignore anything. I don't want to be misunderstood on this point. I am saying that most of the things we think are problems are not. Most of the difficulties we have to face in our lives are structural, are of no significance whatsoever, and evaporate when we come to deal with them.

What I am saying specifically is that before attempting to solve any problem or relate to any difficulty, first, we take it inside. We get in touch with the energy from our own inner Self, and establish ourselves in our own inner work. Doing this allows us to rise a little bit above the particular situation, to a different level within ourselves. As we make this effort, we can actually feel this change in the vibration happening within us. Then, our understanding of what we are relating to will totally change. We won't give it too much importance, and we won't be out of balance with it. Then it is from a different level that we encounter any issue and begin to relate to it. We can start dealing with anything from a deeper sense of self-control, which allows us to dissolve an event, instead of feeding it. At this point, we can start talking. We simply deal with the event, get rid of it, and are finished with it.

In this way, we save tremendous amounts of time and energy, and don't waste it in worrying about essentially nothing. Then we have this time and energy to invest in what has the possibility of bringing us a real return in our life, and an enduring return – a return to the larger field of energy that we are and always have been.

MILAREPA

———

Milarepa was a seriously bad guy. First of all, some people beat up on his family. This made him so angry that he went out, became an accomplished black magi-cian, and did some serious injury to those people. After that, he felt bad. Moreover, since his skill had brought him pride, and in his pride, he also inflicted some injury on himself, he felt pretty bad about that, too.

In due course, he came to a particular Buddhist teacher, a man named Marpa. At the time, Buddhism was not at all strong in Tibet. Because much of the Buddhist teaching was not in Tibetan, but in Sanskrit, Marpa had gone to India various times, learned Sanskrit, and translated many texts. Moreover, he was an accomplished spiritual teacher and master, who was enormously powerful himself.

Milarepa met Marpa, recognized something remarkable in him, and wanted to study with him. Marpa said, "Well, all right, but first go build me a house, and make it in the following way." So, Milarepa went and built the house. Tibetan soil being so rocky, getting the stones out of the mud, and getting wood for the timbers was extremely difficult. It took him four years. So, when he had finally finished, he felt very happy. He brought Marpa to the place, and said, "Here's your house."

Marpa said, "You're a big jerk. You've totally screwed it up. This is not at all what I told you to do, and it's a disaster. Now, take it down, put every rock back exactly where you got it, and start all over again. And do it right, this time." Of course, Marpa knew that if he hadn't done this, the building would have fallen down anyway, so he just kept a step ahead of Milarepa. That's how these things work. To make a long story short, Marpa made him build, tear down, and rebuild that house three more times. For twelve years, Milarepa had to work that hard, without a glimmer of any teaching contact at all. Finally, at the end of twelve years, Marpa accepted him as a student. In fact, Milarepa turned out to be brilliant, and became the originator of several traditions within the context of Tibetan *yoga*.

Milarepa is an example of extraordinary devotion. For twelve years, he did intensely difficult physical labor with little or no support other than his own feeling. On occasion, Marpa's wife would arrange for him to get food, but he received nothing else. Such was the strength of his conviction that he endured all that, and went on to achieve some remarkable levels of understanding, which he wrote and sang about in some of the most beautiful mystical poetry to come out of Asia.

That kind of hard work is extraordinary in itself, and is rare among human beings in general. For someone to have that depth of desire and vision, without any sense of immediate reward and gratification, is truly amazing. It doesn't necessarily take that much work to attain the highest state, but it does take a tremendous amount of devotion.

Unwinding the shroud of illusion that we wrap around the nature of our existence is difficult to do. We spend years reinforcing our most treasured misunderstandings. To cut through them is too much, and few people endure it easily. Rather than learning to sing from the heart of their devotion, they would rather drone out that old dirge, "What's going to happen to me?" There are many *mantras* in the universe, but that one is the most popular, and most people chant it constantly. This makes Milarepa's feat all the more remarkable, and his devotion to growing all the more extraordinary.

A TOTAL COMMITMENT
TO GROWING (i)

People come to the spiritual life and to a spiritual practice for many reasons, but the most basic one is the wish
to know God – to discover the nature of the Absolute. It
is the wish to deepen our relationship to, and our understanding of, what is truly divine in life.

This is not easily accomplished. It is not for the lazy,
not for those who want fast answers, and not for the
faint of heart. It demands resources beyond the ones in-
vested in us as mere biological events. (Luckily for us,
although the Absolute designed us as limited biological events, it also designed us with an override
mechanism, which allows us to go beyond these limitations. Otherwise, we could all probably be stocked on

grocery shelves.) In other words, the desire to know God requires commitment.

This doesn't mean commitment to an ideology; it doesn't mean commitment to another human being. Instead, the desire to know God takes a total inner commitment to growing as a person. Total. If that makes you uncomfortable, I'm happy to hear it. Total commitment to anything is a little uncomfortable, to say the least. Even thinking about it is uncomfortable, let alone doing it.

The other day, someone asked me about devotion stories – stories about other people's commitment. I don't really know that many. One reason I don't is that I've always been too busy trying to practice devotion to memorize stories about it. The other reason is that I find it hard to distinguish between a lot of what I read in spiritual books, and what you find in *Dr. Strange* or *Spiderman* comic books.

One of the marvelous aspects of Indian spiritual culture is all the stories that come forth from the subcontinent about the profound and amazing power of different spiritual people there. Because the true nature of this power is subtle and difficult to explain, the stories get wilder and wilder in an attempt to articulate it, and to give you some idea of what it is. The wildness of the stories then becomes somewhat deceptive. We look at the story of Milarepa, for example. A story like this can seem so remote from our experience that we think, "Well, that's Milarepa and that's incredible, but it's not me. *I* could never do all that."

In another sense, Milarepa's feat was not really one of great, conscious devotion. We may look at it and be amazed, but I'm sure that he was simply facing and taking on what life presented him with, recognizing it as just part of the great effort he had to make to accomplish his end.

So, instead of imagining the extraordinary circumstances you might some day have to confront, and becoming concerned or frightened about them, I would think instead about the significance that lies in making the basic, total commitment to growing. Then I would try to practice *that* every day, no matter what presents itself. Who knows? Maybe in a hundred and fifty years they'll be writing comic books about you!

Spiritual stories aren't the only things that distract people's attention. It truly amazes me to see the lengths of the fantasy in which spiritual people wrap up their heads. The theories they've got running around out there are quite incredible. I hear things I myself never could have thought up. What's more, I personally don't care whether it's the end of the world or the beginning of the world. Knowing who was the greatest teacher of all time doesn't interest me in the slightest. Figuring out how many of the people who have lived on the face of the earth could walk on water, or hop across India on their nose, I find totally irrelevant. This kind of speculation is ridiculous. Only people who can't open up to the drama of their life as it is become preoccupied by and engrossed in theories like these.

I myself don't theorize much. When I do, it has nothing to do with anybody else's circumstances, anybody else's idea, or anybody else's miracle, but rather, with the miracle happening inside myself at all times. This simple miracle is happening in all of us all the time. However, we discover it only when all of our stories, all of our theories, and all of our ideas – and I do mean all – are swept away. At that point, all the concepts on which these ideas are built just release, allowing us to begin to see a simple but dazzlingly sophisticated power within. This is the source of ourselves, of our world, and of everything we can sense.

The total commitment that this requires does not allow us to turn away from our own lives. It in no way diminishes our relationship with anybody else, or with the world. *Au contraire.* You cannot say, "I have a total commitment to growing, so I don't have time to deal with you right now. As for all those people over there, they're too stupid for me to bother with." It's not like that. This total commitment to growing is also a total commitment to living our life in harmony on all levels, and to demonstrating love and respect for all human beings and all things.

Without this, total commitment to anything becomes dry and dusty, and can turn into a rigid kind of fanaticism. Done this way, it makes you demand more and more and more of everyone and everything around you. It isn't that you don't have to be fanatical; you do – but not in a dry and joyless way.

It's like this. In the beginning, we demand much of ourselves. We give ourselves over to this effort to understand God. We do this with a profound love that allows the commitment to mature within. Love and devotion are the indispensable parts of this total commitment to growing. They are what allow it to mature into something beautiful and luscious — to manifest itself as a profound joy within.

We renew this commitment every day, in every situation. We continuously test it, attempting to deepen it on a regular basis. In this way, it evolves into a genuine science, a craft, and an art. It allows us to begin to tap resources within ourselves that go beyond the capacity of our human nature — beyond the narrow band on which our mind transmits and receives.

This total commitment is like a center of gravity. It is an intense point within us, around which the creative energy of Life Itself can begin to mobilize and focus. In turn, a field of grace establishes itself around this focus. This is the best way I know to tell you about it. The presence of an energy field powerful enough to enable us to participate tangibly in that part of us which transcends our humanity is possible only because of our total commitment to growing.

It is impossible to underestimate the importance of this simple, but total, commitment. The alternative is a kind of hysteria which causes us to be consumed by whatever tension is present. Without this total commitment to growing, whatever happens to you is just another slap in the face. Then what does life become? Just a long series of slaps in the face. Even worse, we get so conditioned to it that when we're not getting hit, we think, "Hey, this is a wonderful time!"

Our total commitment to growing is a tremendous source of strength for each of us as human beings. It allows us to take every painful and difficult situation, and to absorb it, digest it, and grow from it. To reaffirm our commitment is to open ourselves to the presence of a grace that will lift us up out of any difficulty and resolve it perfectly in favor of our growth.

I don't care who you are, what you do for a living, or how you live your life. There is not one of us who cannot benefit tremendously from a continuously deepening commitment, made out of love and devotion, to be better at all the things we have to do. No matter where your life takes you, no matter in what form your life presents itself to you, this commitment to growing is the one thing you should always have with you. It should always be there.

For people who do this, there are no questions, there are no answers. There is only divine creativity at work in everything – only the very essence of all that is, continuously revealing and demonstrating its remarkable magic and grace (and I say magic in the purest sense of the word), continuously bringing about in you something utterly beautiful, compassionate, giving, and all-encompassing. When a total commitment to growing is always with you, then all the events that arise in your life are instantaneously transformed into a great blessing.

A TOTAL COMMITMENT
TO GROWING (ii)

A total commitment to growing, as I've said to you before, is not a commitment to an ideology or to a person. Instead, it is a commitment we make to learning and to allowing the essence of life to change us from within ourselves every day. Speaking plainly, it means this: we don't come to a teacher and a teaching to have concrete poured into our head. We certainly don't come to get answers. As far as I'm concerned, not only are there no answers, no rules or regulations, but answers are for dummies – just like rules and regulations are for sheep or cattle – or for vegetables: "You grow here, you grow here, and you grow over there. All in a row."

Life Itself is not like that. We don't discover what is fundamental about our existence unless we stop filling our heads with fantasies, and instead make a total commitment to allowing the creative power of Life to flow within us, work its way through us, and begin to reveal to us its true and essential nature.

A commitment to growing allows us to open and free our minds from attachments to biological, emotional, and ideological patterns so that we can more completely participate in this flow. It enables us to find within the flow itself a tremendous source of strength. Then, drawing on this strength, we can go forward each day to discover the re-creative power of life pulsating within us, observing, participating in, and enjoying its unfoldment into all forms of experience.

This total commitment to growing is, in fact, a liberation. It liberates us from everything that is limited about ourselves and about our experience. It allows us to focus clearly and directly on the essence of these things, which itself is unlimited. In this essence, we experience the pure and silent pregnancy, which is the nature of the Absolute, the nature of the highest Self, the nature of God.

All this translates into a direct, daily action: every day, we practice opening our hearts to feel the flow of energy and the joy within ourselves. We concentrate on these long enough for them to saturate our whole life. We work to become totally absorbed in and by them, allowing them to detach all the tensions that have accumulated in us for years, so that with one deep breath these tensions all dissolve and drain away.

Doing this doesn't make all of life, or everything that happens in it, suddenly understandable. Life remains mysterious. It doesn't make every part of life beautiful. Much remains ugly and brutal. It just makes everything that isn't beautiful bearable, so that we are able to see something wonderful even in what is ugly. We can see that even brutality has its place. It must — it's there. It's not deniable.

Then, because we have the right understanding and make the right effort, and because of our total commitment to growing every day, we don't get caught in tension, confusion, fears, or doubt. Instead of becoming entangled in the various pressures, energies, or complications that we encounter, we simply open deeply within ourselves, feel the inner flow, and allow that flow to organize us in harmony with every single thing we touch.

This is not a way in which we can grasp anything. Instead, it is how we refrain from grasping everything, and allow Life Itself to begin to explain its own true nature to us simply, in a way that is pure, deep, and direct. Only in the presence of this love and joy to which we open ourselves every day can the difficulties, pressures, and different chemistries we encounter be consumed. Love is like an enzyme that breaks down every tension. It makes everything digestible.

By our concentrated effort, we open within ourselves and become established in the simple, pure, essential state from which all events and circumstances emerge. This is not a philosophical abstraction; it is a conscious effort we make to connect to and remain established in the purest essence of Life Itself. Because of our total commitment to growing – our total one-pointed concentration on this inner flow – it opens to us. We discover it to be the essential pregnancy of Life Itself, and we are established in the absolute highest state. This is all you need to know. This is the best teacher of all.

COSTING NOT LESS THAN EVERYTHING

———

To grow as a person will cost you your life – and then will give it back again.

TENSION AND FLOW

———

Tension and flow are different states of the same energy. What is tension on one level is a tremendous nourishment and resource on another level. The difference between them is this: are you resisting?

PATIENCE IS CULTIVATED

Patience is cultivated through a whole process of learning to let go, and of attending to the inner flow. If you practice this, you will notice that the process itself follows a sequence. Initially, there is a period when, in starting to let go of something and to pull your attention away from it, you go through inner chemical changes that you can actually feel.

First, a kind of contraction and resistance sets in. You feel the tension increase and intensify, as the whole pattern you're stuck in condenses to its densest point. While this is happening, you have to hold your attention on it, until it becomes so tight that you think, "I can't do this. I can't do it. I can't do. . ." On the fourth "can't do" – or thereabouts – the whole thing releases, and you find yourself saying, "I *can* do it. I'll be darned."

You learn patience by understanding that there are stages in the flow of energy as it changes from something crystallized to a state of total flow. Furthermore, since there *are* stages in the process, all you can do is sit there, and keep working until it changes. It doesn't happen all at once. It's not a case of instant gratification. When you start to experience tension, the tension itself is tapping you on the shoulder and saying, "Go deeper. Find more flow."

It tells you this to signal to you that the state of the flow within you is not yet able to balance the external pressure that you're experiencing. The lack of patience you experience arises from your bumping into this imbalance. So, you take a breath, you concentrate inside, and you feel a change take place in the flow within. Then, amazingly enough, whatever you're relating to also changes.

SPINNING YOUR WHEELS

Whenever you catch yourself getting all wound up and frustrated, you have to go to work. When you start obsessing, sit down at a piano or a typewriter or start doing something else. Pick up a hammer and learn to be a carpenter. The one thing to do is to have some self-discipline. Take the energy and put it someplace in a simple way, rather than letting it shake you to pieces.

You don't get to pick and choose the outer form of the person you become, but you do have total control over the inner person. To some extent, the two things shape each other, but the inner person is more important. Thus, when you're feeling this energy intensely, you have to discipline yourself: you have to take the energy, express it in simple ways in your life, and begin in a basic way to contribute to the environment in which you're living.

At some stage, maybe you'll be able to do something more creative, but in the beginning you'll just have to pick up a hammer and nails and help somebody else. Either that, or take some initiative to do something on your own in your own physical environment. The thing to remember is that this energy is necessarily a good thing.

Not every creative energy that you're composed of will attract an opportunity for its self-expression, which is also a good thing. If every part of your being found an opportunity to express itself, you would be totally externalized. Furthermore, there must be some frustration in your life, because that subtle tension you feel inside yourself generates tremendous growth. Properly turned under, these tensions and frustrations become the fertilizer of your growth. Properly channelled, they become the power of your spiritual development.

CONTROL

When it comes to having power over other people or events, you have very little – but as for influence, you have all you want. "Power over" means that your will is at work, and because human beings can be profoundly unimaginative, it also means that your capacity to limit yourself and everything around you is in full gear. Only when you really open to, and flow with, other people and situations do you have immense influence on the direction things take. This is different from having power and control, which you don't really want the way you may think you do.

You don't want control over anything because, first of all, control is an illusion. It is an idea based on the feeling that there are actually separate entities – that you and I are essentially different, that we're going to compete, and that one of us is going to win. Of course, a large segment of the population functions in this way, and therefore operates on the assumption that it can control something. There's nothing stopping you from doing this too, but ultimately, the idea of controlling anything proves to be an illusion that fails us, causing us to lose a great deal.

People generally seek control because they're afraid that otherwise they won't get what they want. They fail to understand that you can ask for anything, and if you ask from an honest place within yourself, usually you will get an honest response from a situation. That's always better than getting what you thought you wanted, even though sometimes you'll get that, too.

Suppose you play music. Do you have control over your instrument? No, because there are certain things that it can do, and certain things that it can't. However, the more skill you cultivate, the greater your ability to influence the sounds that the instrument produces. In the same way, it's also true that the more in touch you are with your own flow of creative energy, the greater your ability to relate to the essential creativity of others, and the more your skill in influencing the unfoldment of that creativity.

This is completely different from control, and understood in this way, there's nothing wrong with influence. In fact, all human endeavors are the living and creative mingling of many creative energies and influences, which, ideally, give rise to an outcome far greater than the sum of all the input. No amount of control over a situation can accomplish this.

TAKING DOWN BARRIERS

People often ask about how to let go of the blocks they experience. You have to work at it, that's all. Blocks themselves aren't something you can just drop; instead of focusing on a particular block itself, you work through the larger pattern of which it's a part. Since any pattern is a crystallization of energy, when you focus on it, your conscious attention and concentration bring some heat to the crystallization itself, and start to dissolve it.

For example, sometimes you walk into a room and feel as though you hit a brick wall. You simply don't feel a flow with the people there. Instead, you feel yourself start to close up and pull back. When this happens, you have to say, "No, this is a person I care about," or "This is a situation I care about. I've involved myself in this event, and now I have to take care of it." Taking your attention inside, you demand of yourself the ability to remain present, and to reach a deeper level of understanding.

In doing so, you'll see areas where, generally, you have a great deal of resistance. It may also be that you don't have the exact equipment immediately at hand to understand and deal with the situation, but that the equipment is stored in there someplace. You have to call it forth from within yourself, which takes both effort and concentration.

People usually think that the way to deal with a block is to figure out the real reasons for it. Actually, it isn't particularly important that you understand the reason for any situation because, in fact, there are no "real" reasons. You can spend hundreds of thousands of years in thinking up millions of reasons for why a given condition exists, and when you've reached the end of all that time, you'll still be stuck with the original condition. You may have described it eloquently; you may have researched its roots entirely, but, in the end, all you will have discovered is that its roots lie in ignorance and attachment to fiction. That's all.

When I was in college, I tried this "reasons" approach with my algebra professor. (I had no mental equipment to deal with algebra.) I said, "Look, I had a terrible math teacher in grade school. This nun abused me badly and left me with a tremendous block toward math. Then, when I went to high school, an old geezer of a teacher picked up on this block of mine, and beat on it some more. My brain shut down to math because of all that, and I need a lot of help." He said, "Well, you're going to get it. I'm going to flunk you in this course, and you're going to come back over and over again until you pass it. You'll have a lot of help – as much as you need." I said, "Never mind."

With all due respect, there has been created in our society a whole industry that suggests to us that we can talk our way out of our problems, out of our limitations, and out of doing our work. When you think about these things, you have to understand what it is exactly that you're attempting to do. Either you're building barriers, or you're taking them down. You have to look at yourself to see which you're doing. This requires some introspection on your part – some ability to look at your own behavior. You can't be entirely the victim of your own chemicals. The point is, you have to connect to the higher intelligence within yourself, call it forth, and live from it. If you can pursue this with great concentration, the blocks will take care of themselves.

PAIN AND SUFFERING

———

Nothing is without pain, but there is a big difference between pain and suffering. Pain is when you cut your hand. You don't worry because you know it will get better, and that you'll get over it. Suffering is when you're not sure, and you worry about "What's going to happen to me?" This is the connection between suffering and stupidity.

LIKE TRYING TO DEAL
WITH A CLOUD

────────

My teacher, Rudi, tended to respond to people in the same tone with which they approached him. If they came to him with heaviness, he responded with heaviness. For him, it was a question of self-awareness. He insisted that people try to approach him in his own state – not asking him to come down to theirs, but bringing themselves up to his as best they could.

Of course, Rudi was so fast, that usually just being in his presence for several minutes – even fifteen seconds – would shift your chemistry around. If you came in a little bit cockeyed, first he adjusted you (and you might hear some bones crunch); then, he lovingly answered your question.

Ultimately, this does become a question of self-awareness: if you're required to stop and think about where you are, and about the level of involvement you have in your question – if you have to stop and feel that, and to allow it to change – then, of course, the possibilities for responding to your concern broaden immensely.

The issue is one of where you ask from, and from where you live within yourself. Both of these have everything to do with what you get back. If you live from tension or from need, from drama or from difficulty, then what you get back will be tension, need, drama, and difficulty. If you live from lightness, from joy, and from love, what you get back will be endlessly the same. This is true not only over the long term, but also moment by moment. It is the vibration – the feeling – that you have and sustain within yourself that determines the outcome of any situation on a moment-by-moment basis.

You yourself can tell this. You get into a conversation with someone, and it starts to go wrong. In that moment, you have a choice. (Although most people don't recognize that they even have such a choice.) The situation starts to go wrong, and you fight it. Then it gets worse, and you fight it some more. Finally, it ends up being a disaster. This is not necessary. You can always stop, compose yourself, feel inside, and allow that vibration to change. Then you can speak again, and turn the whole thing in a different direction. You always have this choice.

This is true, too, of your interaction with any teacher – not just Rudi. Of course, Rudi was wonderful in certain ways, but he was so fast and so full of magic, that he could cut all the ordinary corners like crazy. It was always a dazzling event to try to deal with him, or maybe I should say instead, to be dealt with by him.

My saying, "to be dealt with by him" may cause you some concern; you may wonder, "What kind of person was this?" Understand that when you encounter a real teacher – a person with no self-interest, who is established in and operates from love – then it's never a case of your dealing with that person, but of your being dealt with by them. For you to "deal with" such a person would be impossible – it would be like trying to deal with a cloud.

In all of this, the fundamentally important aspect is the feeling with which you live your life, and from which you express your concerns. When I say "to be aware of what you're feeling inside," I do *not* mean being aware of feeling jealous, or happy, or sad. All of that is nonsense, and most people simply use such circumstances in life to become hysterical, or at least, dramatic. Instead, I mean having a sense of the vitality of life and of the simple joy within you; being in touch with that, no matter what's going on around you. The point is that you hold on to that feeling, no matter what. In the end, this is what turns everything around. If you don't do this, you'll just spend more time having the energy of Life adjust you, before it answers your questions.

THE HUM OF THE DRAGON

The *Om* sound is a high-pitched, electrical vibration that I'm sure you've heard – maybe on a quiet morning. There are ten levels – ten different manifestations – of this sound. Chinese Taoists recognize two of these. One they call the hum of the dragon; the other, the growl of the tiger. The *Om* sound is the fundamental vibration of Life Itself. There is no work to be done with it except, when you hear it, to be aware of it.

ATTUNING THE HEART

You have a beautiful heart, but if you don't play it, it goes out of tune.

EXTENDING YOURSELF

Extending yourself beyond your ordinary way of approaching things is not exactly faking it – you learn by doing, and by making an effort. If you don't do this, you'll never learn new ways of handling a situation. So, you make a mistake. Just say, "Hmmm. I seem to have made a little mistake here. Let's backtrack a minute, and start all over again." That's not too hard, is it? It's only when we put our foot down in the wrong place, and then feel we have to defend what we've done, that we compound our mistake with stupidity. That's what makes the mess – not our extending ourselves.

RIGHT EFFORT

———

Many people spend a great deal of time making the wrong effort. What are you going to do? Make a right effort yourself so that you're not one of them. Many people spend their time asking wrong questions. When you ask the wrong questions, you get the wrong answers, and then you think that something is missing. What are you going to do? Ask the right questions, and discover that nothing is missing – and that it never was.

DOUBLE-EDGED TALENTS

People have a real talent for coming up with excuses not to do their spiritual work. The point, however, is that you have to find excuses *to* work, instead of excuses not to. That's all. If making excuses is your talent, then turn it around – everything is double-edged, and every talent cuts both ways. So, use your excuses to make yourself work. Find excuses to grow and to become a bigger person.

Despite the appearance of multiplicity in the world, there is only one essence to all things. If this is so, then what you think of as problems and obstacles to your growing really are not. What you think of as good and bad really are not. There are only forces at work within the field of your awareness in which you must continuously find your balance. If you lose sight of this, then it becomes easy to fall into some kind of self-abuse: "Oh, I'm so weak, I'm so stupid, I'm so afflicted, and besides, nobody likes me!" These can then become wonderful excuses for not working.

Understanding that life is holistic and that all things are ephemeral means that you are not attached to anything. It means that you live your life as an expression of love and respect for the creative power that has given rise to this whole experience. It means, finally, that you give up your excuses.

THE UNACCEPTED DISCIPLE

———

I'm reminded of a story from the *Mahabharata* that Swami Muktananda used to tell about Eklavya, who was the unaccepted disciple of Dronacharya. Now, Dronacharya was a great archer, and a famous man in his time. He was a ruler and a trainer of kings and princes. Eklavya, on the other hand, was your basic low-born person. So, his situation was desperate, indeed.

One day, Eklavya had the opportunity to witness Dronacharya in action, and he was moved by the skill that Dronacharya demonstrated. He went to Dronacharya and said, "Master, I want to study with you." Dronacharya took one look at him, and rejected him, saying, "You're just not good enough."

This went on for a little while. Eklavya asked Drona-charya a few more times, but Dronacharya would have nothing to do with him. Finally, Eklavya built a statue of Dronacharya out of clay and rocks and sticks and stones – a simple statue. Every day, he sat before it in medita-tion. He imagined that the statue was Dronacharya, and he showed it great devotion. Then, every day following his meditation, he would go and practice archery. In time, the grace of the *guru* began to flow to him through his devotion to the statue and from his commitment to learning.

After a few years of this, one day Eklavya was practic-ing his archery. At a distance of some thirty-five or forty yards from him, there happened to be a dog that was trying to dig out a piece of bone stuck between its teeth. Seeing it, and taking pity on it, Eklavya shot an arrow and knocked the bone from between the dog's teeth without harming the dog in the slightest. The dog was frightened and ran off with the arrow still be-tween its teeth.

By chance, it ran past the *ashram* where Drona-charya lived. Dronacharya saw it and was astounded. "That is a secret skill of my own that I've never taught any of my students! How could anyone else know it?" So he sent some of his royal students to find out who had done it.

Eventually, they came upon Eklavya, still practicing his archery. They asked if he'd seen who had shot the arrow between the dog's teeth. Eklavya said, "I did it." Dronacharya's students were shocked. "Where did you learn to do that?" they said. Eklavya replied, "I learned it from Dronacharya."

Dronacharya's students returned to the *ashram*, irate. They shouted, "How dare you not show us the trick that this low-life over here can do? He says that you taught it to him."

Dronacharya was amazed. "Impossible," he said. He went to Eklavya and said, "Let me see you do that again, or something like it." Eklavya demonstrated his skill, and Dronacharya was amazed. He said, "Where did you learn this?" Then Eklavya showed him the statue, and explained what he had done over the years. At last Dronacharya was forced to accept him and recognize him as his disciple.

This is a demonstration of trust sustained over time. Trust of this kind has a tremendous power behind it. When we demonstrate this kind of trust, we have the capacity to learn in remarkable ways. Eklavya could have said, "This Dronacharya is no good anyway, and I'll just forget about it." Instead, he went ahead and concentrated on his commitment to trusting and to growing.

You've heard me say often that it's not the quality of the teacher you have that really counts in the long run. Rather, it is the quality of the student you are that is the essential ingredient in your *sadhana* – your spiritual practice – and that represents the potential for your fulfillment. It is all primarily a question of the effort you make over time.

BEING BOUND BY LOVE

There is only one way to be bound to anyone, and that is by love. Being bound by love is not being bound at all; it's liberation. With my own teachers, I am bound to them by love, and by nothing else. Yet, without the experience of it, how can you ever really speak of being bound to anyone by love, let alone being bound to yourself?

In your own, everyday environment, such love is rarely there, so how can you know about it? It's like trying to talk about sugar when you haven't tasted it, or about Picasso if you haven't seen his paintings. You don't know what you're saying. Only when it comes into your life are you given the chance to understand what complete love is.

This complete love is what you become bound to and bound by. It does, in fact, bind you to yourself by empowering your innermost Self. Then if you look at it carefully, you discover that love like this is all there really is.

SMOKESCREENS AND DUSTSTORMS

———

You may feel that you have a responsibility to a teacher. This "responsibility" is not exactly what you think it is and, as you look back on it in the future, you will see it as something different from what you now think it to be. In my case, did I feel a sense of responsibility to my teachers? Generally, no. Generally, I felt a sense of awe in their company, and a sense of amazement. I felt as though I were on top of the World Trade Center, standing on the railing. There was a kind of precariousness and vulnerability about it. I've found that telling oneself that one has a responsibility is only a way of masking that vulnerability. People find it difficult to deal with it, or with their sense of being exposed. Therefore, they get responsible.

150

The real responsibility here is that of becoming the best person you can be. What does that mean? Well, it will mean something different to each and every person. I refuse to define it, because if you allow me to define what it means for you, then you will only become the best person you can be in *my* image and likeness, and not in your own.

It's not that I couldn't do it. I'm a clever enough person that I could go to the library, and pull out everybody's writings on responsibility and on "what it means to be the best person you can be." I could put all of them together into a book, publish it and sell it, and then spend hours discussing the meaning of it on talk shows. I could probably even make a living at it.

However, there's something that strikes me as profoundly cynical about that whole endeavor. If I'm going to trust and respect you, then I'm also going to have to extend to you the freedom to define yourself, and the love and the nourishment to do so with a minimum of strings attached. Realize, though, that I don't behave this way out of any sense of responsibility to you.

Furthermore, I don't feel any responsibility to the creative energy of Life Itself. Are you kidding? Me, smaller than the tiniest piece of dust floating on the surface of the Pacific, with a sense of responsibility to all that infinity? Who do I think I am? Do you see how a sense of responsibility is just another way to puff oneself up? It becomes a smokescreen, a duststorm; it's a way of clouding over the vastness and the vulnerability that we are as a living event. Instead of really looking at all that vastness, we focus on one minute speck — "Me, I'm responsible. I have ten other specks to pay attention to."

In the beginning, when I started teaching, I was a young person, and I was about twenty-three years old when I was first in charge of the whole *ashram*. At that time, I felt a great sense of responsibility to all the people who were there. As various people left, it tore at my heart. People whom I had loved a lot, and for whom I had thought I was working extremely hard needed to do something else with their lives. How should I have felt about this? Who let down whom?

I feel no sense of responsibility to anybody, and certainly not to the power of Life Itself. However, I do have a profound appreciation for my opportunity to participate in it, in whatever way I can. To the extent that my teachers' presence made it possible for me to do this, I understand that my presence might also promote this in you. But is this a responsibility? No. It's an act of respect and appreciation. True compassion, true kindness, and true service do not come from any sense of responsibility at all. Acts done out of responsibility are not acts of love.

LEARNING

Recently, I read an article about the nature of learning. It presented the results of research that suggested that learning doesn't initially take place in the mind. Rather, it takes place in the muscles and, more deeply, in the chemistry of our brain. Real, physical changes take place during the learning experience. This implies that the more relaxed you are, the more you allow for the experience to penetrate your muscles and chemistry to let that change take place. The ultimate implication of this is fantastic – it means that the highest teaching is not what we articulate in words. Instead, it is simply what we transmit as energy.

Therefore, the conscious part of learning is simply the willingness on your part to learn, which means that you make an effort not to resist the process of change. This permits a flow of energy between you and the source of your learning. In our practice, the transmission of the teaching in the form of this energy exchange is what we call *shaktipat*.

EYES-OPEN CLASS

Our practice includes an eyes-open meditation technique developed by Rudi, which is used in the *kundalini yoga* class when we sit with the teacher. This technique is based on the fact that one of the essential ways in which transmission of the energy, called *shaktipat*, takes place is through eye contact with the teacher. This means that, with your eyes open, in full touch with your senses and in view of the material world, you begin to have a simple, concrete experience of the vital force that connects all things and that binds us together as one. It allows you to sense that subtle inner force at work in even the most powerful of dualistic experiences, in which you ordinarily feel yourself to be a completely distinct entity.

The experience is intended to arouse within you a deep sense of that universal Self of which we are each a part and an expression. It teaches you something about how we are all a demonstration of the creativity and divinity of the Self.

SHAKTIPAT

———

Basically, the point of the teacher's going around to
people and touching them on the head during the *kundalini* class, is to unblock the inner energy centers (*chakras*),
to promote openness within these centers, and to stimu-
late a flow between each of them. Another way of putting
it is that the point of the teacher's looking at or touching
anybody in class is to reach inside the person, to cause
the spirit to coalesce and become stronger, and to arouse
its capacity for change. In this process of *shaktipat*, it is
not your mind but your chemistry that does the learning.
Changed by its exposure to the energy, your whole system is what holds the new understanding. The mind
catches up later.

You see, spiritual teaching and learning don't really happen with words. This is because words are the illusion and not the substance. The substance is transmitted on a very different frequency. It is your ability to still your mind, as well as your ability to open yourself to, and participate in, the flow of this substance, that truly nourishes you, purifies you, brings health on physical, mental, and spiritual levels, and finally establishes you in a state of total well-being.

Words cannot communicate a deep understanding of this kind. We do have the capacity to convey verbal messages to each other, but the words are simply what grip the mind and hold it – distracting you, if you will – while the reality of the interchange is taking place on other levels.

KRIYAS

What are *kriyas*? In the context of your meditation practice, you'll find that the patterns of stress and tension that accumulate through daily living will begin to release. This release may express itself as spontaneous bodily movement, temporary mental agitation, or a powerful emotional response. It's like what happens if you sit on your leg until it falls asleep. When you unbend it, you experience a tingling and burning. In the same way, when you close your mind and your heart and construct barriers within yourself, or when you accumulate feelings of self-rejection, or rejection by others, then these shocks and stresses build up in you. Through your practice, a more subtle flow of energy starts to move in. This

159

is the Breath of Life or, if you will, what's called the *kundalini* energy. When you work to open yourself, it begins to flow more easily through your system. As it flows more powerfully, it rearranges your whole internal structure, just as the tide rearranges the structure of the beach. Then, the universal tide moves in you, and washes away everything that is extraneous.

IS IT POSSIBLE TO HAVE SEVERAL TEACHERS?

───────

Some people wonder, since there are so many teachers and just as many approaches, whether it's possible to have several teachers. This is not really possible. First of all, the style of each teacher is different. But, even if this weren't the case, the main reason – to give you something of a mystical description – is that a teacher is a doorway. Of course, the teacher also has a personality, but this aspect is completely irrelevant and immaterial to your spiritual work. To some extent, you have to get through the personality itself to get through the doorway, but that doorway is the connection to the energy of Life Itself within you. A teacher awakens that energy, and supports its unfoldment in you.

How many doors can you go through at the same time? Try to go through two doors at the same time, and you'll keep on bumping into the wall. It's hard enough to love one person, and to cultivate a deep sense of respect for that one person. If you can do it with one, then you should be able to do it with everybody in the whole world. To try to do it with three or four, or however many, is not so real.

For instance, I have a language that I've tried to evolve. I don't want to use Sanskrit any more than I have to, and I don't want to use spiritual terms that can potentially become clichés. If I catch them becoming so, I change them. I try to make everybody pedal just to keep up. Suppose you take this terminology and go sit with another teacher. Pretty soon, you'll get confused between the other terminology and method, and mine. Then, suppose you go to a Tibetan Buddhist group and you sit there. It all ends up being a case of fifty-two card pickup. You don't know what anybody's talking about anymore, and so you stop trying.

To unfold the potential that exists within you takes a lot of trust. To have a real teacher, you also have to have a real trust. The point is that the trust itself is the teacher, not this bag of dirt of a body here. It's hard to have this level of trust with even one teacher; to have it with many is truly difficult.

I have no problem with your shopping around for a teacher. That's a good thing. But, when you find the right one, stop shopping and get to work. The point is that you don't go from one teacher to another. You do, however, go from one awareness to another. As this happens, you continue to encompass other forms and styles that teach essentially the same thing.

The difficulty for us as Westerners has been, first of all, that we are connected to an Indian tradition, and secondly, that Nityananda was an extraordinarily austere person. How do we fold that Indianness and that austerity into a natural expression of who and what we are today? It's a challenge.

This question of the teacher is the same challenge. It's all really about being connected to the energy of Life Itself. This is the fundamental teaching of Nityananda, of Muktananda, and of Rudi. It's the fundamental teaching of every great saint who has ever walked the earth. What you have to understand is that a real teacher should never limit you in any way. At the same time, you yourself should always – no matter what – be full of a sense of genuine communion and unity toward whatever teacher you have chosen.

As your awareness of this communion unfolds, you'll come to appreciate that all the different forms of its expression are not separate in the slightest. Still, however, you have to start out with a real training, a real discipline, and a real dedication. You have to channel these in a real way, to arrive at the point where you can know and be comfortable with yourself, and where you can participate easily in all of the different forms in which Life asserts Itself. Then, you will also understand that while there are many forms of the teacher, there is truly only one Teacher.

THAT STATE WHERE THERE
ARE NO BOUNDARIES

———

The degree to which you require certainty is the degree to which you also build boundaries and limits around possibilities for your progress. The practice of meditation is one of learning to live in that state within yourself where there are no boundaries. No boundaries means absolute uncertainty. No boundaries means a complete trust.

Then you get to a stage where you become completely comfortable with yourself, and completely comfortable with your life. It's not that you necessarily have a comfortable life, but that you choose to be at ease and in comfort with yourself, whatever your circumstances. Then, no issues arise. You're within yourself, established in your own center, filled with the joy of Life Itself, and whatever form your experience happens to take is fine. Through the love and trust within yourself, you magnetize every experience to take on the form of love, making it wonderful.

BEYOND CONCENTRATION

─────

What you move toward, in your experience of concentration, is the recognition that there is a limit to anybody's capacity to concentrate. This is part of the limitation implicit in the manifesting of any kind of structure. For example, because you appear in the form of a body, you have five fingers – not six, ten, or twenty. This represents a kind of limitation. A tree has a trunk. This structure, too, is a limitation. However, as you concentrate, your attunement also mobilizes and arouses more powerfully the creative energy within you, which is the very essence of divinity within all things.

As you concentrate and arouse this energy, it coalesces and begins to assert itself through and within the indi-

166

vidual field of our existence. That it does so is called grace because it is inexplicable. As you concentrate, you discover that you are no longer imprisoned by the limitations of your own physical or mental energy, but rather, that you are attuned to that extraordinary, divine, creative power which is really concentrating *us*. Then, there is nothing further to be said about limitation. This is to say that consciousness transcends concentration. You could also say that Self meets Self, and there's only Self.

If your mind itself becomes one-pointed, then, from that one point, it is released. The awakening, the release, and the liberation that happen are all really the universal mind. You have seen it in action, and you have also experienced it at different moments within yourself. So, pursue it.

DOES IT PROMOTE
GROWTH?

―――――――

The only thing I would encourage you to think about, in wanting one thing or another, is whether or not what you want really promotes your growth. Does it promote understanding in your life? If you can ask that question of any change you're considering, and get an honest answer of yes, then fine.

However, suppose for example, that it's a case of having a relationship with one person, and after a while, thinking, "Oh, I need a better relationship, or at least a different one." Ask yourself, "Will this different relationship promote my growth?" If you think, "Oh yes," and decide to go off after it, then the other question you have to ask is, "Will this new relationship also promote the growth of the other people involved – both the person I'm going off to be with, as well as the one I'm leaving behind?"

In other words, is your choice only self-serving, or will it promote growth in general? You have to think about any change in this way. If you don't, then the tensions you create in the process will end up getting you into the frying pan. Of course, if you think you're in the frying pan already, you might want to stay there. The fire is worse.

BUILDING THE CENTER

———

Whatever state of relaxation you attain is generally not sustainable unless you build it up. That's why you practice meditation consistently. You do so to find your center, to the point where you're relaxed and able to absorb things easily, and to the point where you have little resistance to interacting with any energy in your environment. Build that center, and strengthen yourself within it continuously. That way, whether things happen quickly or powerfully, whether they represent big changes or simple ones, you're able to participate in them and absorb them. Instead of reacting, you're able to interact with your environment in a progressive way all the time.

170

This takes practice. As long as you look only at the surface of your life, and assume that what you see is what's really happening, then you will always be disappointed. To go beyond this is what takes practice.

WANDERING IN THE DESERT

There is an intermediate stage in your practice, when you're both here and not here. In a way, it's a kind of test. During this stage, sometimes you think that you've fallen asleep. That's all right, too, because in the same way that there are certain frequencies of light which your eye can't perceive, there are frequencies in the energy of Life that your mind can't encompass. As these energies begin to predominate in the field of your awareness, sometimes it will feel as though your mind just disappears. After a while, however, you become increasingly attuned to this frequency, and suddenly it's as though the clouds disperse and light breaks through.

Don't concern yourself about that. Continue to practice, and be aware that this is the toughest stage in which to be because things seem to go so slowly, and because there seems to be so little fire or clarity. It's like the parable of the Jews wandering in the desert for forty years. The intermediate stage is like that.

While you're there, continue to be determined. Your persistence is your strength.

THE COURTSHIP OF
EXCUSES

———

Some people tell me they have a nagging feeling that something is missing in their spiritual practice. My response is that this kind of thinking can present a wonderful excuse for not growing. After all, think what it would mean if there were nothing missing at all. To rise above the enigma of this world and of your life requires a lot of concentration. It requires quieting the mind, and going beyond the idea that something isn't present, or that it's not the time to try, and so on. You simply have to get down to work, which means that you practice intensely.

Maybe you lack confidence in the practice itself. That's fine. You can keep on searching until you find something in which you do feel confident, or until you get tired of searching. Just be aware that, in the meantime, you depreciate your resources. At some stage, you simply have to stop, sit down, and determine that you'll stay where you are until you achieve your goal. At that point, every excuse in the universe will come and court you. Everything you ever wanted will look as though it's about to happen for you. You can embrace it all, but that puts you "back in the high life again."

Many people find teachers and practices deficient in some way or other. Yet those who attain the highest state are those who find no deficiency because the issue is never the teacher or the teaching. Rather, the issue is your quality as a student. If the issue were, indeed, the teacher and the teaching, then it would mean that reality consisted of two things, and not one. A "qualified" teacher is certainly important, but the qualified teacher arises when the student is ready to engage it. With all due respect, if you feel that something is missing, it may be in your own approach. When you become fully present, you will also see that everything you're looking for is right there.

FIRST A MODEL

———

Through your connection with a real teacher, you penetrate the successive layers of manifestation that exist
therein. First, you think that you're dealing with a person and a personality, then with an intellect and a feeling, and finally with a pure energy. So, in the realm of
spirituality, the spiritual teacher becomes first a model,
and then a demonstration of the infinite potential that
unites teacher and student, person and person, mind and
matter, time and space.

THE GREAT AND INFINITE RESERVOIR

―――――

One question that a lot of people ask is, "What are my resources? How do I know what they are?" You don't know, until you look for them. I could give you a list, but if I were to do that, there would be others we'd miss. Besides, your resources are not finite. Rather, they are infinite events, which you organize and mobilize to the depth of your own capability at the moment. The more you work at it, the more these resources become clear to you.

Think of it like this. The energy that made the universe and its abundance – not just the puny abundance of this earth, but the abundance of the whole universe – is the same energy that is within you. So, how rich are you? If you walk around dominated by your awareness of this body, and by your experience of this world, always thinking, "Oh, I don't have this, and I need that, and my life is miserable because of it," then you become like Howard Hughes – totally wealthy, yet completely pathetic. In fact, the great and infinite reservoir of creativity is inside you the whole time.

NONE OF THAT HISTORY MATTERS

———

I have no idea, nor do I think about, what brought me to the life I have. It doesn't matter to me that it brought me to a stage where I wear an orange dress on Sunday morning instead of blue jeans. In anyone's life, the line between where you came from and where you are isn't straight at all. In my case, there's simply no connection – the line got cut somewhere.

You have to understand that none of that history matters. The extent to which you linger on your past is the extent to which you limit your full range of possibility. People often tell themselves (and anyone else who will listen), "Oh, I can't try that new thing. My father did this, or my mother did that to me when I was a child, and

179

it scarred me so much, I can't get over it enough to try what life is presenting me with – even if it might be a challenging opportunity."

You've heard me say that it doesn't matter where you've been, but only where you're going. It's a funny thing about human beings, though. We have some difficult experience in love, and suddenly trust is out of the question. Who do we hurt with this attitude? Only ourselves. If we can't love, and we can't trust, what are we? Certainly not human beings. The part of ourselves we try to defend is precisely the part we should be getting rid of. What is really alive about us doesn't require defending.

When an opportunity for growing presents itself in your life, take it. These opportunities are rare. You don't just walk out into the street and find them lying around. Furthermore, you don't get to choose what the particular opportunity will be, or what it will look like. Usually, it comes in an odd form.

Back when I was thinking about these things, I read all the spiritual comic books. Imagine my surprise when, instead of living in the Himalayas with an eight-thousand-year-old *yogi*, I ended up in New York City with someone like Rudi. The truth is, I didn't think about it. I was grateful that it had happened, and I didn't care what it looked like. I knew within myself that it was true, and I just did it. This is how it is for each of us. When it comes, you have to jump. Whether it's good-looking or ugly, whatever it is, who cares? Just do it.

THE MIND IS LIKE A
LOOSE RATTLE

———

The mind is like a loose rattle. I rarely say, "Quiet the mind." Instead, I say, "Still your mind." The two things are a little different. When you practice meditation, static will continue to reverberate in there. This is not a problem. The real issue is one of how much you get involved in the static that the mind generates over any particular issue.

The mind is basically a dumb thing. Don't pay any attention to what goes on up there – certainly not in meditation, anyway. If you have an issue in your mind, don't think about it, exactly, but simply extend your awareness into the vibration – the feeling – of the issue. If you do this, then some change in your understanding about it can happen. This is somewhat different from thinking about the issue, because you're creating the possibility for the emergence of a bigger perspective, or at the very least, of a different one.

In doing this, you allow the issue to unfold. You could say that you let the knot untie itself. In this way, many issues simply become irrelevant. You come to recognize their irrelevance because when you start to concentrate on them, they just dissolve. It's as if something you had thought to be profoundly important really wasn't in the slightest. At that point, you have the opportunity to open your eyes and say to yourself, "Never mind."

A TREE DOESN'T UNDER-STAND WHAT ITS GOAL IS INTELLECTUALLY

─────

When talking about tasks or goals, think of a tree. A tree doesn't understand what its goal is intellectually; it doesn't follow a rational set of steps that it thinks through one by one before undertaking each of them. In fact, to try to define every single process involved in the growth of a tree would go beyond what a person's mind could consciously articulate. Yet it's a simple thing: the seed takes in nourishment and articulates its creative capacity.

For you, the task is also simple. Just become aware of the natural flow of the creative energy of Life Itself within you. Then that creative capacity and all of the understanding implicit in it will simply unfold before you, because they're already there within you. You're not making anything new. You are studying a living, dynamic event which is already in place. This event does not depend on anything you do – in fact, you depend on everything that it is. Therefore you should look into it carefully, in order to understand fully both yourself and the nature of your task in the material world.

TO REFRAIN FROM
EXPRESSING ANGER

———

By expressing anger to another person, you harm your-self in two ways. First, you block channels of communica-tion with the other person, which, for better or worse, are part of the flow-pattern that nourishes your life – even if that person represents an endless source of frustra-tion for you. Secondly, you contract your understanding of the particular moment. The energy which you express as anger should be more appropriately used to expand this understanding.

If you refrain from expressing your anger, then it be-comes possible for three things to happen. First of all, you have the opportunity to recognize the senselessness of anger, and the need to do something progressive.

Next, you become aware of your responsibility for the difficulty, whatever it may be. This allows you to begin to turn it around inside for a while, after which you can articulate it not as frustration, but as a higher understanding. Finally, in doing this, you can change whatever it is that you've been doing to generate such situations. You can also, at the same time, free the other person from what maybe has been unconscious behavior, developed in reaction to you or to some misunderstanding between you.

Anger is really only a demonstration of some blockage in your own system, and not in anybody else's. Suppose, for example, that the energy in a situation isn't flowing the way you want it to. Instead of trying to force things — which is equivalent to letting this energy build up, get blocked, and turn to anger — you can simply say to yourself, "Oh, it's not going this way. It wants to go some other way. Well, let's see where it wants to go."

I would add two things to this. One is that in every situation, the creative energy of Life Itself has some direction that it wants to go on its own. This is independent of my will or yours. In every relationship and in every situation, you want to try to discover (or at least to become aware of) the direction that the energy itself wishes to take. If you're willing to do this, you then have the chance to learn about the surrender of your own will.

You also have the opportunity to observe the creative power of Life Itself growing and expanding. You witness it expressing something totally natural from within a particular event, and working a kind of magic that is quite remarkable. To cultivate this attitude of openness, and to develop your ability to respond carefully to a situation, may take you some places you wouldn't ordinarily have thought to go, but it will always expand you greatly. As your understanding of this deepens, you will also see that getting angry then becomes only a way of limiting the potentiality that is trying to manifest itself in your life as some great benefit.

GETTING EVEN

Being angry about anything does you absolutely no good, and there's never any getting even. Whatever attempt you make to get even has nothing to do with changing the past. Actually, all that it does is complicate the present and muck up the future.

Basically, any experience that continues to make you twinge is only undigested energy still knocking around in there. Instead of letting it run riot in your system, provoking a response from you every time you encounter something that even remotely resembles the original situation, just relax and absorb it. When you feel it twinging, let go. Don't indulge yourself in it.

If you're willing to do this, you'll find that all of your experience really represents an energy that has the potential to change you deeply. You can learn from everything. It's your resistance to learning, your lack of openness to change, that reinforces the patterns in which you live. This is because that same energy is either building up the pattern that you are or it's promoting a change. It's either reinforcing the crystallization or it's nurturing a big difference within you. You decide every day. Once you understand that you have this choice, the pointlessness of anger – let alone the pointlessness of trying to get even – becomes clear.

TENSION...ENERGY – THE SAME THING

———

Tension and energy are the same thing. In fact, this is analogous to the dichotomy that the Buddhists use with the terms *samsara* and *nirvana*. *Samsara...nirvana* – the same thing; tension...energy – the same thing. When I meet with tension, the first thing I tell myself is that I really want to grow. What that means to me is that I don't get entangled in the tension, but rather that I absorb it and turn it into energy. When you identify with tension, you get stuck. You become part of the obvious crystallization or polarization that tension represents. But when you can take a breath, and draw this tension to a deeper level, or to a point of different vibration within yourself, then all of the tension uncrystallizes. It starts to flow and becomes an energy that lifts you above the level of the event.

It also begins to awaken you to a higher resolution because the tension itself informs you as to how it wants to be resolved, and how it can be resolved in a beneficial way. At that point, you're not imposing anything external onto the situation; you're simply taking it to a deeper level and responding to what it has to tell you.

I explain this to you because this is the basis for understanding what growth is. Growth represents the release of tensions, freeing the energy to disclose its secrets and the secrets of your own nature to you. Instead of getting stuck and polarized in tension, tell yourself, "No, I want to grow. I really want to grow." This prevents you from identifying with a stupid situation.

The decision to grow continuously changes your focus. In every situation, you're there to grow, period. You're not there to fight, to analyze, or to intellectualize; you're not even there to talk, necessarily, but to grow. When you confront tension, first you make this inner effort. Then, something dawns on you, and you find that you can do the right thing.

ALL SUCH TRANSITORY
STATES

———

Depression is, in some ways, worse than anger. It's certainly trickier. Still, you grow only by rising above your depression and continually connecting to the deeper energy – even when the purpose, the focus, the direction, and the outcome of this energy are not apparent to you. Since anger, depression, and all such states are totally transitory, your work is to rise above them – to become established in a state in which you feel the inner flow, and experience the total sense of well-being that emerges from it, even when you don't know where your next meal is coming from.

The important thing about this is that in making this effort, you discover something about nonattachment.

You begin to appreciate the power of trusting Life, and the power of trusting God. Ultimately, it doesn't matter what the outcome of any event is. What matters is your ability to be above these little moments of uncertainty. How can you truly appreciate a happy ending without them? Otherwise, it's all just a short story.

SUCH A VITAL PROCESS

Spiritual growth is such a vital and creative process that it renews itself continuously. This is what enables you to keep picking yourself up and starting over again in your work. That's what I had to do. It may be that the main difference between my beginning training and yours is that I wasn't embarrassed or self-conscious about having to start all over again ten times every hour. I didn't mind. If I was a dummy, so what? I figured, if I do this enough, then I won't be a dummy forever. That's why I'm still doing it.

INTENSITY AND DISCIPLINE

Intensity and discipline are what you use to let go of anything to which you feel attached. You do this by turning
the intensity of your attachment back inside yourself,
and with that energy, in a disciplined way, you let go.
How else can it happen?

Then the issue becomes one of who will be the
master – you, or the intensity? You must learn to master
it. One thing you can do is to focus that intensity within
yourself on your own heart, and tell yourself deeply and
honestly that you want to let go. Keep telling yourself
that, and feel what happens. See if you don't feel some
kind of change take place inside you. The more you cultivate that openness, the greater your capacity to let go,
because instead of being attached to things and circumstances, you're attached to the energy of Life.

A HANDFUL OF RABBIT PELLETS

The shocks and the stress that you naturally accumulate as a human being living your life tend to stay with you in your muscles. It's similar to what would happen if someone took a baseball bat and hit your arm with it. The muscles would go into shock, and would stay that way for a long time.

We experience many levels of shock continuously. Furthermore, we also usually live in the midst of the shocks and tensions we've held onto from our experiences of twenty years before. This is called *karma*. It means that our whole life is wrapped in a veil of things that occurred long ago. The pain we experience in growing is the ripping of that veil.

Human beings are funny, fragile creatures. Most of us have a handful of rabbit pellets that we carry around and protect like mad. If anybody tries to take our pellets away, we want to kill them because we think our pellets are all we've got. We don't understand that whoever's trying to take them may also be trying to give us gold – we know rabbit pellets, but we don't recognize gold, and we're afraid of making a change.

Change, itself, is painful, but that pain is a wonderful thing. Releasing the nerves that have essentially been asleep all that time is like a liberation. As they wake up, they may jump around a bit, but this, too, passes.

As these stresses and strains begin to dissipate, and the parts of you that have been asleep start to wake up, you need the ability to stay open. Without the determination to do this, you're likely to react to these inner changes, and just stop your work. Then, you're in an even harder spot than before because you not only have the original stresses and strains, but also the cynicism you've added from thinking that spiritual practice doesn't work.

NOT GETTING LOST IN
THE OPENNESS

——————

The challenge in working to be open is to keep from getting lost in the openness. This involves paying attention to two things. One is to being really open to all the possibilities that present themselves within any given situation. The other involves not forgetting what you were doing when you went into the situation in the first place.

A perfect example is when you're working on a project. Someone gets upset about something, so you sit down to discuss it. In the context of trying to be open and to work through the difficulty, you forget about the original purpose of the whole thing, and end up saying, "Oh, it's all right. Never mind." Then, you tell yourself that everything is fine. For a while, everything does seem fine, and everyone is friendly – until you start relating to the same goal again, the same person gets tense again, and everything comes back full circle.

In your effort to be open, you still have the responsibility to keep your attention focussed on your goal, and to remember who you are. It's one thing to be open, gracious, and hospitable to people; it's another thing to buy into every kind of business deal they bring your way. Saying yes to everything in the name of openness just doesn't work. In fact, it's not being open at all; it's being irresponsible. The challenge is certainly to be open, but in the end, it's also to be clear about what you're doing, and what your life is about.

THE GREAT SAINTS WERE ECCENTRIC

————

Many of the great saints were eccentric in the extreme. The fact of the matter, however, is that this has nothing to do with anything. From all great beings you learn that personality is irrelevant. You're not with them to understand why they do the things they do, but to tap into the power from which they do them. If you try to figure out what they're doing or why, your brain will just get broken – which is not entirely a bad thing, of course. This, too, can be a stage in the process, if you keep going.

BLOCKS

If you're still thinking about a block you're experiencing, then you're only making it more powerful. Whatever the problem you think you have, working on it directly only diverts more of your energy into it. Try, instead, to focus on the big picture, and to establish yourself in a more productive pattern of living. If you pay attention to this pattern – the big picture – eventually all the blocks will fall away on their own.

WORKING DEEPER

———

Working deeper refers to your ability to concentrate on more and more essential elements of the process of Life Itself. This implies something total. What I mean is that working deeper is something you do everywhere. It isn't just sitting down in meditation and feeling deeply within yourself. Rather, it is the point of any spiritual endeavor to become a deeper person in all ways, and, in all of your endeavors, to be more attuned both to the essence of your own Self and to the essence of the particular endeavor. Working deeper is a question of balancing these things, and of continually taking care to maintain that balance – no matter how heavy the two ends of the scale might become.

202

RESPONSIBILITY

You can pay attention to the question of responsibility, but just how much you have to buy into it is a whole different matter. To think that you have a responsibility to others is a bit wrongheaded, because once you think of something in those terms, you're likely to find it burdensome. Personally, I don't think in terms of responsibility. I don't feel that I have a responsibility to you, or to anybody. At the same time, I do have a great love and appreciation for the incredible, creative power of Life. I find any opportunity I have to be involved in this – to participate in it or to promote its expression in anybody – tremendously exciting.

To promote such opportunities in the fullest way, you have to learn to balance between responding to the immediate circumstances that confront you and sustaining the work you already have going on. This means that you have to be somewhat careful. Still, this is different from responsibility.

Furthermore, the balance has to be light. You have to try to determine where your participation is genuinely useful, and where it is merely a matter of wasting time. Do what's useful, but don't waste time. For example, if your aging relatives need you to do something for them, fine. If they need to know that you care about them, let them know. If, on the other hand, it comes to your sitting there in the living room listening to them complain about one another, then you don't have time for it. At that point, think of them as friends who eat only pinto beans for dinner. You want to leave right after the food is taken off the table because you're a fervent believer in clean air, and feel a keen responsibility to preserve it.

SEND YOUR CHILDREN ON
A LONG JOURNEY

There's nothing you can do either to control or to protect your children, your friends, or any of the people you
love. Of course it's painful to stand by, watching them do
every kind of stupid thing imaginable and getting themselves into every kind of difficulty. I have the same feeling. I constantly watch people I love jumping off bridges,
beating their heads against walls, and playing stickball in
traffic. There's nothing I can do. It's enough to tear your
guts out.

Still, it's not your job to protect the people you love.
It's only your job to be there when they've taken a beating and they need you. It's your job to promote the healing after the damage is done. In fact, sometimes a little

205

damage is a good thing. It makes a person stronger. In any case, the bottom line is that you're not going to stop them from doing what they really want to do. If you push it, you'll only cause the information to go underground. There's an old saying in the Orient: "If you really love your children, send them on a long journey." You have to let other people make mistakes.

In the context of your own spiritual practice, you can't be concerned about making mistakes yourself. They're a good thing, and nobody will ever reject you for them. The only things that people will get upset about are your arrogance or your egotism. These things can be a problem; mistakes are not. Furthermore, you don't learn unless you make a few — so feel free to, and let other people do the same.

THE EXPLORATION OF
PURE ACTION

———

Service is an opportunity to explore, free of all the complications of self-interest, the essence of activity itself. When there's no self-interest involved in what you do, then a lot of the chemicals in your system don't get engaged. When those chemicals aren't present, then your ego doesn't have its usual relationship to the activity. It's a wonderful opportunity to explore pure action – to be aware of it and to feel it. If you do this for a while, then slowly you understand something not only about pure action, but also about its source.

It is in serving, at whatever level, that you begin to understand what true love is about. In understanding *that*, you begin to live from it. In living from it, you find a freedom from tension and pressure, and a freedom from sorrow and suffering, which is difficult for people to imagine really exists.

IN A TREMENDOUS, GRAND INTERCHANGE

———

I was thinking the other day that when most people think about growing, they operate with a frame of mind oriented by the idea of cause-and-effect. Many of us, in the recesses of our unconscious, have the powerful predisposition to think in terms such as these: "God created the world out there with a purpose in mind, which is working itself out everyday. We're not only a part of this big plan; we're also struggling to find our spot in it so that we can do our job, be a good person, get our paycheck, and get out of here." This perspective requires that we get directed and organized, and that we become successful. This is also what we often have in mind when we talk about "growing."

But wait a minute. What if there isn't any big plan at all? What if *what* you are is just fine? In that case, what happens to failure? In that case, maybe there's no such thing as success. Do you see the powerful set of assumptions that can bias your thinking about growing?

Suppose you go into the forest and see the myriad forms of life functioning all at once in that environment. There are great trees and fragile ones; there are grasses, vines, and flowers; there are thousands and thousands of organisms, all consuming and being consumed in a tremendous, grand interchange. In all that, who's successful and who's a failure?

We think in terms like "success," "failure," and "goals" for a number of reasons. For one thing, our biological imperatives to eat and reproduce contribute to goal-oriented thinking and behavior, because eating and reproducing are specific objectives. What we recognize less often is that maybe all of this is simply a small part of a much bigger pattern intrinsic to each of us. Maybe we're looking at only a minute part of the total pattern that we are. This means that growing is understanding more and more of this total pattern.

When you recognize this, then, instead of having your attention locked up in one of the most minute aspects of that pattern, suddenly your mind breaks free, and you wake to the total pattern itself. Everything is still in place, but instead of being trapped in this small part and not understanding its relation to anything else – instead of being fearful about what's on either side of it – you open to the whole thing. Suddenly, all the small things that were so distressing before take on their true significance. At this point, you have a true perspective on them, and the whole question of success and failure becomes irrelevant.

MUSHROOMS AND MOTOR OIL

The thirst to make money and the thirst for spiritual growth are one and the same in that they are both desires. There is, however, a big difference between motor oil and water in terms of their capacity to satisfy your thirst. If you're not sure of this, try drinking a tall glass of motor oil. You may never feel anything again. My point is that neither this – nor anything else material, for that matter – will ever satisfy your spiritual thirst.

There's no problem with making money. In fact, I think it's fine. In our culture, some degree of material stability is necessary because we don't have the institutions and patronage systems that allowed the great religious traditions of the East to set up events where people could come to live, practice, and study. Therefore, it's necessary for you to be financially established in some way.

After that, however, there remains a deeper issue — the search for meaning, the search for truth in your life, and the search for honesty and integrity within yourself. This is an ongoing process, and one that you should continue to respond to all the time, no matter what else is going on in your life. If you do so, then making money becomes just one of the areas in which you give expression to your search for, and your unfoldment of, mastery within yourself.

People often feel that they should come to spiritual work out of a purely selfless desire. But you see, almost nobody comes to this whole process with an utterly selfless desire, because people who are utterly selfless don't pursue anything in the first place. They're established in the highest state already, so what is there to pursue? This means that worrying about whether or not you're selfless in your desire to pursue spiritual work is not the issue. Simply start out by pursuing it. You may not even know exactly why you're doing it. When I first met Rudi, I think — inasmuch as I've ever reflected on it — that my motives were as selfless as possible. I really did want to grow, and I didn't care what it took. I also never took much time to worry about it, and I don't feel any need to do so now.

You find out how selfless you are in the process of pursuing your spiritual work. The different blocks and tensions that you encounter, as well as the different tendencies to get stuck in your head or in your emotions will, themselves, point out the areas in which you need to work to attain selflessness. Until you stop resisting, they'll keep finding ways to show you this. If you continue this work, you become selfless; if you don't, your selfishness endures. But nobody begins selflessly — why should they?

On one level, it's only because you come to see the enduring and practical value of selflessness to the unfoldment of all areas of your own self-interest, that you continue to pursue it. On another level, to become selfless means that you transcend your own limited self-interest, in order to begin to respond to a deeper interest to which you're connected. Eventually, you recognize the total interdependency of your individual self with the Self of the whole of Life. Then, you become selfless in the small sense, but quite filled with Self in the large sense.

I was walking through the woods the other day. A thick layer of asphalt had recently been laid down on the road. Amazingly enough, right in the middle of the road some mushrooms had burst through the asphalt. There were none at the edges — just there in the middle. The asphalt was a few inches deep, but the mushrooms had powered their way through. Mushrooms! Something you could step on and crush.

That's the power of Life. It's the force of the inner Self, pushing its way through the crystallization and tension, the rejection and the insecurity, the fear and the doubt that we imagine we are. It's that Self which leads us to respond to the deeper issues in the first place, and to undergo the necessary changes in our limited self-understanding.

Certainly most people have all kinds of personal, limited interests going on. However, you cannot sustain your spiritual work over time unless you deal with that selfishness and eliminate it. That's the only thing that will keep a person going. Otherwise, you become so constipated by selfishness that you fall away completely from the desire to pursue any kind of spiritual endeavor. That leaves you with only material pursuits, and then you're right back to drinking motor oil.

GOALS

———

Goals are important for mobilizing our resources, and for directing our energy concretely and specifically. In some ways, they also give us an important source of information about our performance. At the same time, they present equally powerful problems, some of which are directly related to the spiritual aspect of our development. This is because the goal-setting process itself is based on a profound misunderstanding of who and what we are. As a result, the goals themselves are also misdirected.

There has to be some flexibility in our thinking to allow us to adjust our goals as we grow. (In any goal-setting activity, hopefully, we ourselves do grow from the

215

process.) As we grow, we're going to make changes. There should be room for these in the system from the beginning, because when we start out on any project, there's no way we can know everything about it from the beginning. For example, in spiritual work we often start out with the goal of becoming enlightened. However, as we grow we discover that to have such a goal is, itself, a part of the problem.

Materially, goals are essential; spiritually, they're an obstruction. There might seem to be a contradiction here, but that's not exactly the case. Rather, an evolution occurs. First, you think of goals in terms of the foundation you've built in your worldly life. Then, you begin to think of them more according to an orientation that you evolve psychologically. Finally, you reach a state in which you are no longer attached to any kind of goal-orientation at all. This doesn't mean that you become indifferent to anything, but rather that you become detached. It means no longer thinking of enlightenment as a goal.

It's a bit difficult to keep all of this organized – but that's part of the balancing act in spiritual work. It's something like being in two places at once when you're really nowhere at all.

BURNING IS PART OF
THE PROCESS

It is true that your efforts to refine your understanding can work against you if they're misdirected. How will you know? Continue with your practice. I assure you that Life will give you continuous, uninterrupted feedback about how you're doing.

As you refine your understanding, you may have the experience of burning. This is not an indication of misdirected effort. Rather, it is part of the process of refinement, in which the tensions, the thickness, the dimness, and the misunderstanding that we are – both materially and chemically – burn up, and are transformed into pure, conscious light and energy.

CHOICES

People abuse themselves in many ways. They forget that they have a choice – as do you. You can stop abusing yourself at any point. The linchpin here is whether or not you want to grow. If you really do, then you take any difficult circumstance that you encounter, and ask yourself, "How could I have handled this better? What does this tell me about myself? What does it tell me about the world in which I live and operate?" You always have this choice.

SPIRITUAL COMMUNITIES

We note that spiritual communities have endured over the greater known history of the human race. There must be a good reason for this. For most people, it's hard to get a good perspective on themselves if they are attempting to do spiritual work on their own. Unless they're exceptionally strong, the possibility is much greater of succumbing to some moment of loneliness, and acting out in a foolish way. The existence of a community serves as a balance to this. It acts, on the one hand, as a support, and on the other hand, as a restraint. It gives feedback about the different programs that a person might be considering as possible courses of action. This is a good thing.

Some people worry that this can become oppressive — that they will be forbidden to do what they want with their lives. However, a real community should never limit your options in any way whatsoever. In fact, a spiritual community should exist to promote the development of every individual within it. It should promote each person's experience of the Self, and his or her capacity to articulate that experience in whatever form he or she might choose. At the same time, the presence of the community asks the question, "Is this really the Self that you're seeing, and is this really the proper, or the finest, expression of it with which you can come forth?"

Human beings, in general, are party animals. I don't know how much anybody is intrinsically a loner. Indeed, a loner of a human being is a rare event. I can think of only one individual, Nityananda, who was so strong that he could have been categorized as a loner in this sense. He was surrounded by thousands of people all the time, yet he was like this.

Since being filled with love — filled with God — also means that you serve other people, how can you be alone? Right there, you're talking community again. It might be nice to be alone, but it doesn't work out that way. (So, it may be that people who think of themselves as loners aren't thinking in quite the right way.)

The reality is that you're always interacting with other people, whether it's one-to-one, or one with many. Then it becomes a question of how fast you can change gears. To live in a community successfully means that you learn to change gears quickly.

220

This, too, is a good thing. The world itself is continuously throwing every kind of oddball energy at you. If you can't get above it fast, then you find yourself in the middle of it before you know what you're doing. First you're in the middle of it; then, you're underneath it. This means that a spiritual community also has a training element in it, all of which is a support to your practice.

EXPECTATIONS

————

The point of any serious growing that we do – or of any serious effort in that direction – is to bring us closer to reality, and to free us from our expectations and our desires. If you're really interested in learning about this, then you have to pay attention to what's actually happening in any given situation, and not to what you want to have happen.

This doesn't mean that you have to deny or repress anything. If you have a certain expectation, it doesn't mean that you should try to push it back, because to be completely free of expectations is not possible. Rather than trying to induce some artificial mental state in yourself (which will only end up confusing you about what you're doing), pay attention to what's *really* happening, independent of your expectation. Pay attention to the flow of energy within yourself, and to your relationship with your environment and the people therein. Watch the patterns.

Don't listen to what people say to you – don't even listen to what you say to yourself. Just pay attention to what happens. Recognize, too, that developing this ability is a long-term project. If you get a few jolts along the way, you shouldn't be too disappointed.

You'll find that the biggest problem with developing expectations is that you tend not to know when to cut your losses. You invest in a relationship or a project, and you expect something to happen. Having put time and energy into it – and perhaps money or other resources – you want it to take place in a certain way. Even though all of the signals may be there to tell you that the thing isn't going to work out as you had thought, you keep going. Then, when it sinks, you're angry at somebody – maybe yourself.

It's a good thing every now and again to reflect on the projects you have going on, and the goals you've established, to be sure that what you imagine to be happening actually is. To be able to reflect on these things honestly means that you can never be afraid to walk away from anything that really isn't going in the direction you had hoped it would. This doesn't mean that you necessarily walk away; it does mean that you can't be afraid to do so because as long as you're afraid, you won't let yourself see the whole picture of any situation.

There is, of course, always a whole raft of intervening steps that you can take before walking away, as well as a boatload of approaches to any problem you have with a project. What makes all the difference every time is your ability to face what's really going on, and your ability to be detached.

HIGHER ENERGIES

People sometimes ask whether there are higher energies beyond human comprehension, and whether we experience these through mind and matter. First of all, "comprehension" itself refers to an activity of the mind. Secondly, there are many energies that you won't be able to wrap your mind around, but there are no higher energies in the universe that aren't within you. Since the highest energies are within you, it is by surrendering – by taking your attention away from the material part and stilling your mind – that you begin to experience all of these higher energies within yourself and in your own life.

PAIN IS GOD'S LOVE

─────

For many years, I've had the thought that pain is my best friend and my constant companion. (For that matter, it's everybody's constant companion.) Rudi used to say that pain is God's love. The one thing I find about pain is that it has never lied to me. It's totally honest, whereas plea-sure – the other shadowy companion with whom we try to associate all the time – lies to you constantly. What-ever pleasure tells you one moment will be different the next; whatever pain tells you today holds true for always. You simply don't want to hear what it has to say.

Pain is the source of real love in your life. This may sound confusing because of certain assumptions you hold about pain, but look at it from another perspective. I'm

226

not talking about pain as darkness or gloom. It may not be the cutest friend you've ever had in your life, but it's not a bad thing. How is this possible?

When you can really open your heart to pain – when you can accept pain into yourself without flinching or resisting – then you're a strong person. If you can live with pain quietly and simply, then what can ever happen to hurt you? What can happen to rob you of your dignity, your intelligence, or your integrity? Of course, when most people see pain coming, they throw away their brains. (Actually, it's integrity that goes first. Honesty goes second, and everything else goes after that.)

Life itself is a brutal experience. The point of learning to deal with pain is that you're then not reduced to the level of brutality that surrounds you. Slowly, by your acceptance of pain and your ability to live with it, you discover the hidden possibilities that exist within yourself and all around your life. Think about it. Pain tells you to go beyond your limitations in this moment, and in every moment that follows. If you can get beyond pain, then how can you ever have the notion that you have problems in your life?

I'm not talking gloom and doom religion. This is not fire, brimstone, and judgment. It's just a simple understanding that pain is really your friend, and not something to be avoided. When you feel it coming – when you feel it reaching out to touch you – instead of pulling away, turn around and face it. When you can look pain dead in the eye, then you can also see God.

THE MISSIONARY URGE

People are always repeating what I call the *mantra* of stupidity: "What's going to happen to me?" This *mantra* causes you to become contracted and your mental and emotional barriers to become increasingly thick and dense. By focusing all your energy on protecting what appears to be your own self-interest, this *mantra* is really little more than a way of extending and cultivating your own ego. Growth, on the other hand, revolves around the issue of getting beyond your ego, and serving something greater.

Any time you connect to and participate in a broader field of energy in the world – whether in a relationship, in a series of relationships, or in some project – you engage reciprocal reactions among a number of forces. The degree to which you demonstrate your understanding of service, by trying to think about and serve the long-term best interests of all these forces, is the degree to which you get beyond your ego.

By service in the world, I'm not talking about going to Africa and converting people, or going to India and trying to change the people there in some other way. In fact, I have a real concern about any missionary urge that people express, when it means going out and trying to change other people. This is still a case of proving that your own way is right, and of trying to get the world to be more like yourself. When it takes this form, altruism becomes one of the most obnoxious forms of pride, exceeded only by missionary zeal. Neither of these represents true service. I think, instead, that to serve means you change yourself. Many occasions for service of this kind present themselves in your immediate environment. These are among the most powerful and important opportunities you have as a human being to learn what it means to serve.

Understanding service – looking into yourself, and from the deepest place in you, really trying to connect to the best interest of each and every one of your activities – slowly dissolves your ego. In the long run, it causes you to understand that this long-term best interest has nothing to do with the part of you that you call "I" – the ego. Ultimately, this is what takes you beyond the question of "What's going to happen to me?"

INTEGRITY

Integrity comes from two things: from being true to your own life, and at the same time, from having a great respect for the life of whatever it is you are relating to. This is true whether you are talking about the life and the purpose of a business situation, of an artistic event, or of a personal relationship.

For example, in a business situation you have to consider two sets of interests – those of the people with whom you work, and those of the people to whom you sell or for whom you produce. This is not a complicated issue. The best interests of both should really be one. To sell somebody something they don't need, and to do so knowingly, doesn't demonstrate much integrity. If you work with people who push you to do so, then it shows that they don't have much integrity either, and that maybe you should look for someplace else to work.

You will flourish in any environment that encourages you to cultivate your understanding of integrity – especially if integrity already functions as a part of that environment itself. If you don't have that respect and appreciation for your own life and for the life of the other person, then it becomes difficult. You end up not with an inner sense of correct behavior based on a respect that arises from within yourself, but with an ideology that has a set of external rules and regulations. At that point, we are no longer discussing inner integrity, but an externally imposed system of ethics and morality.

WORDS (i)

———

I have a respect for words and their power, but I understand that words have meanings the way that icebergs have meaning. The real volume is not seen, the real depth and vastness not understood.

USELESS QUESTIONS

To ask, "What's wrong with me?" is a useless question. If you ask this of yourself, you come up with a list of answers that extends from here all the way to the river. Maybe further. It's simply not a helpful question to ask in the first place. Instead, ask "What's right with me?" If you can begin to discover what's right with you, this is so extraordinary and compelling that all the rest flushes away immediately. You may be conditioned to ask "What's wrong with me?" but honestly speaking, when you take what's wrong with you and put it against what's right, you can give a simple answer: nothing is wrong. Nothing at all.

DESCENT OF GRACE

The word *shaktipat* is a technical term, meaning "descent of grace," or "transmission of the energy." Think of breaking up the ice on a frozen stream. It isn't that the flow underneath ever stopped, but with the ice broken up, things can now also float downstream along the surface. The whole flow opens up. The experience of *shaktipat* is something like this. It doesn't add anything to the system; it simply arouses and organizes what was there previously in a way that it can now flow and function unobstructed.

I was thinking about this the other day, recalling the first time I ever looked at a painting and actually saw it. When I was young, I'd look at a piece of art, but without *seeing* anything. The first time I really opened my eyes to what I was looking at, I recognized in that moment that there was more to this event than I had ever appreciated or understood before.

Shaktipat is something like this, too. It's like opening your eyes to the power of Life within you, and suddenly beginning to see what you really are. It's a moment that signifies the possibility for tremendous growth, but also the need to do a lot of work in getting there. If you stop doing the work, then it's like the stream – everything freezes over again. This, in itself, becomes painful to live with, because once you've had the experience of *shaktipat*, how do you forget about it? It's like Einstein's theory of relativity: to change one thing is to change everything.

HAVING LOVE FOR
ONE PERSON

—————

Someone asked me recently whether there was any room in our spiritual awakening for loving a particular man or woman, or whether it was necessary to give up such relationships to pursue spiritual work. I would put this a little differently. Whether you are involved in a relationship with another person or not, the aim in this or any situation is to have some understanding and some insight into your own nature.

"To understand," of course, can sometimes be interpreted as having an intellectual understanding. That's not what I mean. Rather, I mean "understanding" as a palpable awareness and a living contact with the pure essence of Life Itself within you. To have that living contact with yourself means that you also have it with everybody else. Then, if you spend your life with one person, that's fine. Having love for a specific person in no way limits you from also having love for everybody else. Living with one person doesn't limit you from sharing things with many people.

The only thing that you're going to have to give up — which is always the real question in the process of growing spiritually anyway — is your tensions. You will have to renounce, transcend, and sweep out all of these. Giving up tensions is what represents the real possibility for having a long-term, continuously loving, honest, and living relationship with another person. If you don't give them up, then chances are that any and all of the relationships you have with other people will eventually become stuck.

When you see these patterns of tension emerging within you, recognize that there's work to do. Ultimately, it is this work which allows you to develop insight into your own nature. This must be the starting point for loving any other person.

ALL BARS WERE EXACTLY THE SAME

———

People wonder about how to cultivate a yearning to grow in a spiritual practice. They also worry that if they *do* cultivate it, they may miss out on having an exciting life. Personally, I developed an intense desire for spirituality when, after having lived an intense life on the other side of the coin, I recognized that it was dull, dreary, dense, and dim. Indeed, I had exhausted myself on that particular plane by the age of twenty, having visited more bars than I can remember in five states over a period of five years. At that point, I realized that all bars were exactly the same, and never went back to another one. I knew that there had to be a much better way to live.

238

The issue is this: if you really have a desire to live, and if you truly value life, then, even though you might go down one trail for a little while, whatever trail you travel will lead you to an intense desire to grow as a person. Caring deeply about anything ultimately leads to caring about Life. I tell people simply to do good work, whatever that work is. Care about the quality of your work in your science, your study, your profession, or your relationships. Do well. Don't be lazy. Care deeply. If you care, then ultimately, you must come to an understanding of the immense importance of spiritual growth.

TECHNIQUE IS A BRIDGE

Technique – such as the practice of different types of breathing in meditation – is just the bridge you use between the tension and crystallization you experience on the one hand, and a state of flow on the other. As you become more and more established in that state of flow, technique is less and less apparent.

For example, suppose you're dribbling a basketball on a court. A certain tension exists between you and the hoop, because you know that you're supposed to get the ball through the hoop. Since that doesn't happen easily by itself, you practice a lot, and you work on your technique. You remember to bring your feet together and to take the ball in both hands. You put one hand under

240

and one hand on top. You bring the ball all the way over your head and release it. Then, you keep on doing that, over and over again.

If you do it enough, you get to the point where you're somebody like Larry Bird for whom there doesn't appear to be any technique at all. The man doesn't even look at the basket; he just flips the ball. He can get it into someone else's hands, even when the other person is running down the court – and do it from behind without even looking. He can hit the basket in the same way. Where's the technique? There's no technique – just pure understanding.

A lot of practice went into building that level of sensitivity and attunement, and a lot of work goes into sustaining it. Bird goes out before a game and walks over every square inch of any court that he's on. He figures out how many steps it takes to get from one end of the court to any point where he might want to make a shot. He also knows where all the soft spots are on any court. If he sees another player cutting in to dribble on one of them, he positions himself to make a steal, because he knows that the dribble won't be true. He's ready.

Practice starts out as technique, but it becomes pure consciousness. If you start with technique and get stuck in technique, then there comes a point at which that technique will get in your way. Larry Bird isn't thinking, "Now, both feet together..." In fact, if you look at the way he plays, it appears as though he breaks every rule. He makes jump shots without even setting himself, and I once saw him shoot from his hip with his left hand –

while running at full speed. Here is someone who has mastered his craft and turned it into an art.

A lot of practice and technique also went into building that degree of awareness. In this sense, technique is necessary. If you look at Zen archers, you see the wonderful way in which they shoot at and hit a target without ever looking at the target itself. However, you weren't there for the twenty-five years that they were standing there hitting trees, the sides of the temple, and the floor right in front of them.

Your practice is also work. It just happens to be the essential work of your human existence, and the most important thing that anybody can do in their entire life. It happens to be the effort that you have to make in order to create the fundamental ground from which you can really enjoy, value, and treat both morally and responsibly, every person and event that enters into your life. In learning to cross over onto this ground, technique is nothing but the bridge to making your life into an artistic act of profound attunement.

WHEN THERE IS BEAUTY
WITHIN YOU

——

When you understand that the great source of satisfaction exists within you, just as you are, then you don't need to bother with anything else. Very simply, when there is beauty within you – when there is love within you – then love grows up everywhere in your life. When there is giving in you, then giving grows up everywhere in your life. Then there is no need to manipulate or change anything, because there is already something utterly amazing in you as you are. I won't say that it's perfect, in the Judeo-Christian sense, but I will say that there is perfection there.

You have, in this life, so few moments together with the people you love. For that matter, you have so few moments in general. Maybe you'll see thirty or forty more seasons, and then you're finished. How, then, do you have time to manipulate anything or to worry? It's really more a question of appreciation. Let's simply appreciate deeply the moments we have together, opening ourselves to them and participating in them. That's enough. Nothing else is needed.

WHEN THE PAST COMES UP

—————

All people have within themselves a powerful creative force that is limited by a painful past only if they allow it to be. Furthermore, every single person in some way had a painful childhood. It's remarkable that all human beings, no matter what their circumstances, can report pain and suffering as a part of their past. This is the nature of life.

Life hurts. You don't need to have reasons for that, it just does. The real test for us as human beings is our ability to absorb that pain, to transcend it, and to allow the expression of our life to be something beneficial.

Instead of getting caught up with pain from your past, you have to focus on accomplishing something in your life. In the end, the real thing to accomplish is to grow as a human being. If, to start the process, you have to focus on some outside goal, that's all right, too. Begin by doing something that means something to you. If you can't find something that means something to you today, do anything. Don't make excuses to wait before starting. Then what's meaningful can come.

To think about the past — even as close a past as what happened when you walked into the room — is nowhere. Already it doesn't exist, so don't let it take hold of you. Sometimes, lacking the proper fire under us, or lacking the right kind of strength to move forward in our lives, we fall back on thinking about the past.

Yet, even if there is nothing external to move you, every person has the ability to lift himself or herself up and go forward. Then, all this consideration of pain — even present pain — proves worthless. It is only your way of becoming (or staying) constipated. The first thing to do is to make a real commitment within yourself to rise above it. When it starts to come up inside of you, push it away.

Furthermore, all of these feelings — all of the past, for that matter — are blurred, because memory is an extraordinarily sketchy, selective, and highly-edited piece of videotape. The older it gets, the more peculiar the perspectives can become. Often, we remember only what we want to. We have the ability to shape facts and figures in such a way that even if we perceive things with complete honesty on the front-side, our continuous reorganizing of the data on the disk bends it into something hardly recognizable on the back-side. We take past circumstances and weave them around a particular tension that we currently feel. In this way, we create something that sort of happened, but that also sort of didn't happen, to justify our inability to move ourselves forward.

After a while, it becomes like steel netting. The longer you live with it, the stronger it gets. In reality, the past is like a phantom; you should blow right through it, and forget about it. It's *now* that's important, and the simplest way to deal with right this moment is to open your heart. If it doesn't want to open up for you, knock at it a little bit. Push it.

We become accustomed to being defensive and closed. We get so stuck in self-rejection that we don't want to take the risks. We don't want to open up, and we don't want to feel the flow of Life Itself. We find it too frightening. However, this condition is equivalent to not living. Personally, I would rather be in tremendous pain and be alive, than be blocking pain, shutting down all systems, and functioning on the level of some geological feature. So, when the past comes up, instead of getting involved in it, take a deep breath and say no to it. Flush it. Then, tell yourself that what you really want is to grow, and remember that pain is simply strong energy.

HOW SPIRITUAL PEOPLE
REALLY LIVE

In close encounters with me, or with any teacher, you will run up against that teacher's eccentricities. In other words, you'll meet that person's humanity. For example, you may – with all due respect – occasionally see me pick my nose, which you may find totally contradictory to spirituality. The important point here is that it's not. Some people will make something like this the reason to find fault and to leave. Others will take it as an opportunity to recognize and experience that even when something like this is happening, the energy is still present. From there, they will begin to re-think their understanding of themselves.

It's important to begin to connect to and feel this spiritual presence, even in a form that sometimes seems outrageous. This experience gives you the opportunity to absorb directly the appropriateness of your own outrageous behavior. In this way, you begin to recognize that every aspect of your life is all right. You begin to be comfortable with your own self and with many of your own peculiarities. Then, you can relax and be full of self-acceptance. Once you stop trying to judge and criticize yourself and, instead, accept yourself just as you are (but with full self-awareness and a commitment to sustaining love and joy within yourself) then the possibility for real growth begins.

Generally speaking, we have no understanding of how spiritual people really live. We have only our own illusions, and the spiritual funny papers with which we support those illusions. I've been fortunate to have lived closely with at least four great saints. I can tell you about it, but it's encountering it directly that teaches you the main lesson. So, when you encounter the humanity of the teacher, the question to ask yourself is what will *you* do about it?

THREE GRAINS OF RICE

People sometimes evaluate a teacher or a practice on the basis of whether or not they are "supportive." Thinking about my own experience, when I arrived at Rudi's in New York, I suppose you could say that I got no support at all of this kind. But, in a way, I didn't require any. I was so grateful to have found Rudi that I didn't need anything else. When I got to his place, everybody was working, so I said I'd like to help out. They gave me a job hauling boulders out of the basement. Then, when I finished that, they sent me over to a sub-basement on Broadway and Spring Street, and said, "Here, change all the pipes." For entertainment on weekends, we went up to Big Indian – a retreat center we had in the Catskill Mountains – and worked there all day.

The point is that "support" as it's often understood is not exactly the issue. The real issue is the connection you experience with both the teacher and the practice. The degree to which you experience that connection, and sense in it the possibility for a real learning or transforming experience will show you whether or not the particular teacher and practice are what you want to pursue. Then you begin to discover that these support you in an entirely different way from what you thought you needed.

I'll tell you something else. The more powerful the experience, the more difficult and demanding it's going to be. If anything, it's not going to seem supportive at all. Nobody at Rudi's ever said, "Oh, we hope you're feeling O.K. – not too tired," or "How you doing? Are you up to it?"

There were only five of us who lived in Rudi's house. The senior student there used to come home at one o'clock in the morning. If there were three grains of rice in the sink, he'd wake me to clean them up. He was already awake – he hadn't even gone to bed yet – but he'd haul me out of bed and say, "What happened to the sink? Get over there and clean it up!" What did I say? I said, "Yes, sir," and cleaned the sink. I could have fought it. I could have gone to Rudi and said, "What's with this guy?" I didn't, because I didn't want to introduce any tension. I wanted only one thing, and that was to grow.

Personally, I believe that the most powerful learning opportunities, or the strongest energies in which you can participate, also represent the most difficult challenges.

They break down your resistance instead of reinforcing it. They don't support your inertia; they crunch it. These energies are going to reach way down inside of you, and pull out things you never knew were there. Ultimately, that's what allows Life Itself to support you. That's fantastic. That's what you want.

FALLING INTO EVERY TRAP

———

Self-sabotage in your spiritual practice comes from a certain lack of discipline and commitment. The fears that arise in the context of your practice challenge you to develop this discipline, and facing them is part and parcel of your work. You respond to them by maintaining your work. Your fears may still be there, but they don't have to stop you from doing what you are doing. That's why you practice meditation techniques every day. To some extent, this allows you to relax and to focus on your work, which then allows you to deal with your fear and uncertainty. These do not have to sabotage you.

Actually, the biggest issue of self-sabotage comes later: you do your work, and an inner power starts to grow in you. It may start to move your muscles and skull around, to shift your vertabrae, and even break a few bones. This is to say that it changes your entire chemistry. But let's say you manage to hold it together through all of that. Then you start to discover that you have some spiritual power or gift that has emerged from within you because of your intense effort. You start to think, "My God, I can do something unusual. I think I'll do it for my friend over here." Maybe you even cause something to happen. "Oh! That was terrific! Now I think I'll do it for that friend over there." A week later, you're doing it on street corners for whoever happens to pass by. At that point, you're not doing spiritual work anymore; you've become an entertainer.

Do you understand? Thinking you can do anything like this is one of the biggest traps you can fall into as soon as you get over the fear part – and it's much trickier than dealing with any kind of fear. It's much more subtle. It's also an egotistical, wrongheaded notion that leads to your undoing.

In spiritual work, as in any field, there are plenty of traps to fall into along the way. What's more, it's a given that you'll fall into all of them. In itself, that's not such a bad thing. Indeed, if you're lucky, you'll fall into all of them, and then find your way out. Finding the way out is the lucky part. That happens because you really care about what you're doing.

Actually, falling into every trap is wonderful. There's nothing wrong with it. Indeed, it's the only way that you can really learn. I could write a whole manual

254

on traps inherent in spiritual growth. You could memorize it and become an expert on it, but it would mean absolutely nothing to you until suddenly you found yourself in the middle of a trap. Then you would say, "Aha! That's what he meant." There's nothing wrong with self-sabotage in anything, as long as you get over it. It's the getting over it that's the big problem. However, not getting over it, in the long run, simply demonstrates a person's lack of commitment to his or her own growth.

DO EVENTS SIMPLY HAPPEN?

―――――

Do events simply happen to you, or do you create them? I don't think that it's necessarily useful to try to figure this out. However, there is one thing I would do: I would take responsibility for all of it. Until you're in a position to make an accurate distinction, assume that it's all you. Then, at least, you can do something about it.

WORDS (ii)

Words are temporary and ephemeral, and most people never say what they really mean. Consequently, words are a double-edged sword. At times, they have the capacity to bring truth and light, but mostly they spread deception. People often characterize their behavior, circumstances, and events in blatantly inappropriate terms, and words are the vehicle by which they convey the deception. As a result, the extent to which you take other people's words seriously is the extent to which you set yourself up to be deluded in some way. You know very well that when you really want to *hear* someone, you don't listen to what he or she says. You don't listen to the words. You listen deeply into the person, and go beyond the words.

This is not to say that words have no significance; it is to say that they are not the most significant aspect of any event. You know that to say, "I love you" is one thing, but that to communicate such love can be something fifty million miles away. Anybody can say, "I love you," but how many people have the capacity to demonstrate it truly? The main thing to ask yourself is this: "Do I have that capacity?" If the answer is no, then you had better start asking how to acquire it. You don't need to acquire the love itself because that's already there, but having the clarity, the stability, and the strength to communicate it with depth, over time, is a horse of a different color.

What I mean is this: mouth to mouth is fine, but heart to heart is better.

PEOPLE LIMIT THEMSELVES
WITH GOALS

———

It's a good thing to have goals, and to use goals to channel your energy in the beginning. However, if you're really going to grow, after a certain stage, goals should not be the limits that define your creative expression. In fact, goal-oriented behavior can fall by the wayside entirely. Suppose, for example, that you're a musician. At some stage in your pursuit of musical excellence, after you have mastered a certain set of skills, music is no longer an act of technical expression, but rather, something that flows deeply from within you. There is a union of you, your instrument, your technique, and the feeling that you have. The point is that your whole life can be that, too.

259

People who live a goal-oriented life are likely to reach the end of their lives feeling a certain kind of sadness. They'll find themselves saying, "I didn't accomplish my goals," or "I wasn't a very good person." However, when you focus on growing, and not on goals, then the real potential of the different experiences you encounter begins to show itself, because your view of an event is no longer limited by what you want out of it.

The irony is that, generally speaking, people don't want much out of life – especially not when compared to what's available. What do I mean by that? I mean that few people are willing to work hard enough to achieve their potential. It's much more comfortable to say, "Oh, I can't do that. It's too hard."

In this way, people limit themselves with goals and with a goal-oriented mentality. They say to life, "I don't want the whole Swiss cheese; I just want a tenth of a pound."

Life is always trying to say, "Here, take the whole thing!"

"No, I don't want the whole thing. I just want this much."

"You can give it to your friends."

"I only want this much."

"It will feed a thousand people."

"I don't want to feed a thousand people. I only want to feed myself."

When you no longer have a goal-oriented mentality, then you also don't think anything is either too hard or too easy. Opportunities simply show themselves, and you see them more closely for what they are. Finally, you understand that there is something vast within you, which is the foundation of your life and the essence of your purpose here, and that everything important about this whole experience you call Life is inside of you, and not outside. Then, at a certain stage, you recognize that there's no such thing as "outside," and that there's nothing toward which to direct your goals in the first place.

NOTHING TO FEAR – JUST CHANGE TO BE FACED

The way to deal with fear is to cultivate your inner strength. As you learn about the vast energy, ability, and potential hidden within you, and as you unfold these, the big difficulty in your life is no longer one of overcoming the fear of anything. Rather, having begun to unfold this energy, the difficulty becomes one of keeping up with it as it goes roaring on. Your life becomes a progressive expression of the energy, and you experience only a deep awe for the power of Life Itself. In a way, that could seem to be a sort of fear, but it's not really.

In general, there's nothing to fear – just change to be faced. Still, that's the toughest part. It's why most people would rather defend and stay in a bad situation that they

know, than reach for the possibility of new and better –
but totally unknown – circumstances.

In a way, this is a difficult matter for me to discuss
personally, because I've never had the good sense to be
afraid of anything. I think that you have to take that attitude. Ultimately, the big fear for most people is that
there will be too much work. But think about it: if you
let fear stop you, then where will you be? I think that you
have to take the attitude that there is nothing to fear –
not even the work.

PATIENTLY HURRYING

You have to work and make an effort. Your job is to push yourself. At the same time, you have to be confident, and trust in the fact that there is a process. Implicit in the idea of a process are both movement and a period of time. What do you want to do? Do you want to sit back and wait for everything to happen? If you do, you could be kept waiting for a thousand years: "There's no rush here – this person is willing to wait. Let's bring the energy over there instead, to all these people who are *really* in a hurry." It's better to be in a hurry, but with patience.

ALL PSYCHOLOGICAL
STATES ARE FALSE

───────

As you persist in your practice, slowly you come to understand that all psychological states are false, Of course, this is not most people's understanding these days. The many therapies floating around teach them, instead, to indulge in analyzing every possible psychological state: "I'm feeling this thing," or "I don't feel that thing"; "I like myself," or "I don't like myself." However, a fundamental principle in *yoga*, and in every spiritual practice, is that all such states are false. Each of them is transitory, and what you get entangled in today will pass away to a new entanglement tomorrow. The real question is to free yourself from every entanglement.

To find happiness, you must understand that all psychological states are false. Then you can begin to look

beyond the parade of psychologies that present themselves for your entertainment, and begin to feel more
deeply. I don't mean "feel" in the emotional sense – "Oh,
I'm feeling kind of twitterpated today!" I mean, to reach
within yourself, and to have a palpable contact with the
very ground on which all these psychological states
parade themselves. I mean, to begin – through this direct, palpable experience – to understand the nature of
that ground.

In this way, you establish yourself in a simple, pure,
one-on-one relationship with the ground of everything –
the source of all Life. The various psychological states are
merely the secondary effects – the gasses and smoke, if
you will – of the fire which is the source.

When you pay attention to your direct experience of
the fire, then you realize just how superficial all the soot
and cinders thrown off by that fire really are, and how
little they can teach you about the fire itself. At that
point, you no longer take them seriously. You no longer
live your life reacting to and acting out the particular
psychological state that is prancing around the parade
ground that day.

As you work to understand this, slowly it becomes impossible to hold on to any identity or state as permanent
and real. It becomes impossible to think that you really
understand anything, or that you really know anything as
a permanent fixture of reality. You become aware of this
slowly, even as you continue to deepen a different kind of
knowing – a knowing of spirit. This is a knowing in
which you also don't know anything, but in a different

way – because spirit is no thing at all, yet the essence of all things. You live comfortably with the fact that you can know nothing and everything at the same time.

Furthermore, in terms of spiritual work, you come to see that nothing you think you know about yourself – that is, about your personality – really has any significance at all. People sometimes get nervous when they hear this, because they are so used to thinking that they *are* their personalities. When I say that personality has no real significance for spiritual work, they think I mean that a person who does spiritual work inevitably becomes some kind of zombie. I want to make it very clear that this is not at all what I mean.

I mean, instead, that you have to re-think what you mean by "personality," and look at ways in which this notion restricts you more than it frees you. "Personality" is only a way of drawing boundaries and making limits, but these are precisely the limits that don't promote your growth. To open yourself fully to the energy of Life, and to allow it to happen within you and within your life, means that you have to begin to think of yourself as encompassing much more than the boundaries with which you've learned to define yourself. This takes nothing away from you at all – except those artificial boundaries that have prevented you from recognizing the true reality of what you are and what you know.

In the end, everything reduces to a single state of total well-being, in which individual facts, issues, and points of view all lose themselves in a panorama of points of view that manifest like lights in the night-time sky.

Look up some night, and tell me which star is better than any other.

The more you hold on to what you think you are, the more you limit yourself. The bottom line is that you are so much more than you can ever understand by looking in a mirror, or by evaluating yourself based on your experiences in a given day. It's like trying to describe an onion by the first layer of its skin.

Ultimately, all that should concern you is that you grow and become the best person you can be. Then, feeling something or not feeling it, liking yourself or not liking yourself – all these become nothing more than elephants in the parade.

WHAT'S REALLY GOOD
ABOUT YOU

————

I want you to meditate on what's really good about you –
even on whatever is wonderful within you. Don't just
think about it; try to feel it. If you can do this in a simple
way for even a few minutes, then practice feeling it more
strongly. Do this each day. If you'll think about this and
meditate on it every day, you will grow tremendously as a
person, and your whole understanding of yourself, of
your life, and of the creative power that binds these two
together will change completely. Then, whatever the
form in which you live your life, whatever the form in
which you express yourself, whatever inconsistencies or
"imperfections" there may be, you will find a great sense
of peace and a great ability to bring benefit to those
people whose lives your life touches.

ETHICS AND MORALITY

———

I have an aversion to discussing ethics and morality if the purpose of the discussion is to judge others or to decide what is appropriate for somebody else according to your own perspective. True ethics and morality never have anything to do with anybody else, *ever*. They don't even have to do with formal behavior. Rather, they have to do with the respect that you demonstrate, through your ordinary, daily behavior, for your life and for the lives of other people. Furthermore, for each person, the issue of ethics and morality is really an issue of becoming worthy of trust – worthy of trusting yourself and worthy of being trusted by others. This is the whole thrust of the issue.

TO JUDGE A PERSON

To judge a person's performance is one thing. To judge the person is something different. You can be utterly open and loving with a person, and still say, "My friend, your effort here just doesn't make it." Sometimes this is the most loving and respectful thing you can do. If the person doesn't take it in this spirit, it's not your problem.

Sometimes when you say hard things to people, they may go through a reactive stage. Don't get entangled in that; don't feel the need to reach out, or to hold them. If you do that, you allow yourself to be brought down to a level where you end up saying, "Oh, everything's all right, and I didn't mean it" – which is a lie on both counts. You did mean it, it is *not* all right, and you just put yourself in a bind.

Let them go through it. If they boil over to the point where the real, capable person in them emerges and says, "I understand, and I'm going to try to change. Will you help me?" then you can say, "Yes, but these things you have to get done." If you get caught up in the boil-over, all you get is to be called names. Still, you can survive even that. I've been called more names than you'll ever be called, and I'm still fairly cheerful.

SUPPOSE YOU HAVE
TWO CHILDREN

———

Suppose you have two children. You're doing something with one of them, and the other comes and wants your attention too. What do you do? You have to produce more energy. You have to work not only harder, but smarter, so that while you're doing something with one, you can also hold the hand of the other. It's really a matter of learning to relate to two things and be in two places at the same time.

Being with the younger child requires one kind of chemistry; being with the older one requires another. Instead of changing gears rapidly back and forth from one thing to the other, you have to learn to be in both of these places at once. This means that you work to

273

feel the vibration of the one child – to feel into her, connect to her, and participate in her – even as you nurture the other.

It becomes a question of consciousness and of your ability to tune into both children at the same time, so that no matter what's happening on the surface, you're not distracted by it or caught in it. Instead, you're relating to the depth of the event. Once you do this, in a few minutes – however the situation started out – it's got to change. Instead of reacting to the surface, you're now relating from a deeper place in yourself to a deeper place in the child. You'll find that, in a little while, she'll feel that nourishment. When she's satisfied, she'll detach herself, wander off, and be content. It's a matter of your not getting caught in appearances, but continuing to relate first of all to your own resource and then, from your own energy, to your children.

In this way, you take care of jealousy, because you make sure that there's no sense on anybody's part that one is benefiting at the expense of the other. It shouldn't take too much thought to see that this is also true of any situation in which you have to give your attention to more than one person at the same time.

GET QUIET

———

The real culmination to the part of your spiritual practice that involves effort comes as you begin to recognize those moments when your mind is going off track and you are able to switch it back on track. The end-point of this effort happens when we develop a level of self-awareness that allows us not to take eighteen side-trips into various tensions in the first place.

In learning to do this, you'll find that the mind is the real obstacle. The trick to it, when you recognize some tension starting to build up, is to become still. When you start to hear the "Does he or doesn't he?" or the "Did she or didn't she?" then it's time to get quiet.

IN SACRED TRUST

The essence of the relationship between a student and a teacher is trust. It's not that the relationship is *based* on trust, but that it *is* a trust – a sacred trust. This is something you will have to work to understand, because only rarely does a person walk into this relationship and immediately trust it in the deepest possible way.

Let me put it somewhat differently. The relationship between a student and a teacher has, in a broad sense, two basic levels: one of these is like the connection between a patient and a physician; the other is a deeper connection, that goes beyond even that. In the first connection, a physical and emotional healing experience happens based on the flow or exchange of energy between the teacher and the student. This flow itself isn't exactly physical, but it *is* a force. Thus, it does have a certain quality of physicality. It brings about a certain level of wellness in your life, makes you feel better, and enables you to deal with the tensions of your life in a simple way.

In themselves, these healing experiences are wonderful things, but they also point beyond themselves to demonstrate the presence and the worthiness of your connection to an even larger energy field. They are part of the proof of its power; they are also part of the reassurance you require that the openness and trust which you are cultivating are grounded in something real. The deeper connection is related to, but also greater than, the physicality of the healing experience. It is what offers the real opportunity for learning.

If learning is a process of multidimensional chemical change in the body, this is certainly true of the teacher-student relationship. This deeper connection with the teacher is like an immersion in an energy field. It allows for a profound, chemical transformation to take place within you, dissolving layers and layers of tension, and virtually stripping a veil from covering over your awareness.

It's important to understand that this is really what's going on, because people tend to think about this relationship in fairly superficial ways. They think about it as though the relationship were an electrical connection that gets plugged and unplugged because of some exchange. Yet to imagine a teacher getting angry, result-

ing in a break in the relationship, is not only ridiculous – it also demonstrates an extremely superficial
trust in the first place, as well as a superficial contact
with the true depth of the relationship itself.

What we identify in our minds as the cause of a break
in this field of trust is really just an expression of that
superficiality. It demonstrates the degree to which we
were not connected in the first place. You never have a
simple cause-and-effect connection between an event
and the breaking of any relationship, because breaks in
any relationship never happen all at once. Rather, they
build up over a period of time, until some event becomes
the actual manifestation of the break – you might say,
the excuse for it – but even this is not correct because
the relationship was already broken.

People see in the teacher what they want to see and
what they are looking for. When they are filled with fear,
then they see things to be afraid of in the teacher. When
they are perpetually intimidated and filled with doubts
and mistrust, then they see intimidation and things to be
doubted and mistrusted.

Such people usually end up saying that it's somebody
else's fault, when it's not – failing to recognize that this
is also how they are living their lives in general. It doesn't
occur to them that if they were looking to see love, trust,
and respect, then that would be what they'd find. The
point is to sweep aside all these mental and emotional
trips, to get rid of the fear, drop all the issues, and simply
connect to, be nourished by, and slowly start to live
from, the energy of Life Itself.

You may feel that the personality of the teacher makes it difficult to develop this connection, but the personality of the teacher is no more significant in helping you with this work than your own personality. Of course, it's always easy to see the deficiencies in the personality of someone else, and you're already familiar with the ones that you think exist in your own. Indeed, you can wrap up a lot of your energy paying attention to both; in the end, you get nowhere.

This makes it crucial for you to understand that personalities are meaningless in terms of the resources that further your spiritual work. Once you understand this, it frees you to get to the heart of the matter – the deeper connection and a more profound trust, both of which bypass the superficial aspects of anybody's personality.

Only when you develop a capacity for profound trust can you rise above the limited perspective that most individuals bring to their lives; only then can you deal effectively with all the tensions in your life. The power of trust within you is what gives you the strength to go beyond the superficial levels, to see beyond the tensions, and to begin to deal with life simply.

Not only will the trust challenge you to rise to it, and to live from it every single day, but many things will also happen to you to challenge the trust itself. Everything that does so is wonderful. All of it is your tension breaking out and manifesting itself powerfully, giving you the opportunity to face it and deal with it – hopefully, even once-and-for-all (or at least for the time *before* the once-and-for-all).

Furthermore, you have to be worthy of the trust in your life. If you think about this trust in petty terms, then the potential depth of the experience will never be fully called forth from within you. At the same time, to have a trust means that you understand there are limits to every connection, to every structure, and to every event– just as there are limits to our own ability to extend ourselves. You must constantly be alert to those limits, learning to respect and live within them. Otherwise, you begin to abuse the trust by manipulating it.

You don't get anything for nothing, and you should get over any idea you might have that you can. All the benefits that you hope for are based on your inner effort. You work for them. As they unfold, you become responsible for them. That is the only way. Because you are willing to work and to pay the price with your effort and caring – because you take great care of your inner commitment to growing – you begin to understand what a trust really is, and become worthy of having that trust be alive within you.

Trust like this is a powerful event. You have no idea how powerful. It will challenge you mentally and emotionally in every way, but it also has the capacity to transform you in every way. When you nurture a seed, it goes through many different changes.

In the same way, as you are nourished and start to grow in trust, you will go through many changes and will sometimes be surprised by the things that come out of you. But if you are sincere in your trust, then no power in heaven or earth can break it. Finally, it matures into a complete and total state of well-being, of fulfillment, and of unity with God in Life Itself.

This is a process that takes on more than an individual expression. Think about the early Christians and their reason for coming together, or the early Buddhists and the importance of their communities. Think about our own community. Something special happens in a situation like this. There is a truly remarkable nourishment here which is based on trust, comes out of trust, and extends to trust.

The essential ingredient that allows this trust to grow and flourish is respect. That may come as a surprise to you, because it is true that we tease each other a lot here. It keeps the atmosphere light, and keeps everybody laughing about their own and everybody else's faults. That's a good thing. But underneath it all, there is something powerful and sacred. No matter how much we joke around and have fun, no matter how light and simple we keep things, you must never lose sight of, or fail to appreciate and respect, the very sacredness that allows it all to work for you in your life.

The center of this sacredness and this trust is your relationship to the teacher. We have to learn to trust something, and we usually feel that we have every reason not to trust ourselves. So, you start out with a teacher – you trust another human being. You practice and practice that trust, and gradually come to trust many other human beings. You cultivate your trust, and allow it to grow inside you until you mature, and until the trust grows to reveal itself as nothing more than the creative energy of Life from within. It develops into a complete trust in yourself, and finally, you trust in Life Itself. At that point, the teacher – seen as a separate teacher – seems like a dream, taking on an illusory appearance. Then you understand that the teacher was always inside you.

At some point, that will happen to you. Until it does, don't try to fake it. I meet lots of people – in fact, whenever anyone gets angry with me – who do try to fake it: "Oh, the teacher is inside; it's not that idiot over there!" There may well be an idiot over here. I don't know. But this trust so profoundly transcends personality that it makes any discussion at that level absurd. If you can't open yourself to trust and to encompass another person within its flow, then where will you be, if not in the prison of your own limitation? This trust encompasses *every* personality – even every potential personality. It's almost exhausting to think about the amount of work that it requires, but it's also wonderful. You have to understand that the trust itself doesn't limit you in any way. Certainly, however, you can limit yourself in relationship to it. Think about this, because in terms of your potential to grow, it is *the* issue.

This openness is an effort, a quest, and a challenge that you will face for much of your life. In search of such a trust, finally you will be freed of every limitation. You will be freed even from your limited self and from your own ego.

The foundation of self-mastery is trust.

FORGETTING THE FUTURE

———

There were two things, finally, that I cared about – my reputation and my future. When both of these were ruined, I had an extraordinary spiritual upliftment. In everybody's life, once these things are finished, then there's nothing else to talk about.

The point is that you have to forget about the world. When, finally, you are completely finished with what other people think about you; when you are finished with having to know exactly what your future will be, then you can be completely centered in this moment. You can be completely at peace with yourself and with Life Itself. That's the beginning.

LEPRECHAUNS AND THE
TEN THOUSAND THINGS

In your spiritual work, you'll find that a certain tremendous joy arises as you experience the awakening of the energy of Life Itself. Then, reality sets in as you see that it's also a lot of work – a lot of *real* work. But even that's all right; you simply have to be determined.

Rudi once described the quest for fulfillment as something like grabbing hold of a leprechaun – it tries to elude you by changing into ten thousand things. Sometimes it's sweet. Then, it tries to romance and seduce you. At other times, it will try to bore you or to exhaust you or to frighten you. It does many different things to you before finally, it breaks off and gives up its treasure.

284

FORGET THE EXCESS BAGGAGE

———

If you think of yourself as a holistic event and of the various tensions you encounter as different kinds of attachment, then your work, your practice, and your life can only be a progressive experience. Forget about the excess baggage beyond that.

Make an honest effort every day to live from within yourself, to experience the fundamental flow of the creative power of God within you, and speak as best you can from your understanding of yourself and your life, as one with Life Itself. Practice nonattachment. In other words, when tension comes up between you and somebody else, let go of it.

To be on the path toward spiritual unfoldment is to forget about your problems. It's not to have guilt, but rather to drop your limitations completely. Cultivate the best part of yourself, and don't spend time with anything less than that.

BEYOND STRUGGLE

———

Your work really begins when you release struggle. To let go of struggle initiates a change of vibration within you. This change puts you in touch with the flow of Life Itself, which is essentially what you are. To cultivate your awareness of this flow is your real work.

When you're in touch with the flow of Life and feel your heart and mind open, you'll note that a certain presence starts to assert itself. This presence changes your physical chemistry, your feelings, and your mind. It is the spirit itself, starting to inform you about yourself, about it, about Life, and about God. It's a simple work.

Usually, however, you're so involved in struggling that you can't extract yourself enough to do that work. This is one of the reasons to practice *hatha yoga*. *Hatha* stretches and changes your muscles, and starts your breathing going in a different way. You can also practice breathing exercises and meditation techniques to promote relaxation and awareness on a bio-energetic level. These things permit your physical system to relax and allow you easier access to this inner spirit.

The point is to drop the struggle. If you have to drop it five hundred times a day, that's all right. No problem. Keep dropping it. If you keep doing this, eventually it will stay dropped. Then, your real work can begin.

IN THE FORM OF THE TIDES,
IN THE FIRE OF LOVE

————

One of the most important things you can come to understand from practicing meditation and from cultivating your awareness of the creative energy inside of you is that the significant reality of your life unfolds within that inner creative force. The natural growth that you work for happens within you yourself. It doesn't happen outside of you or anywhere else; it's not even in anybody else's hands but your own.

To say that what you're working for is in your own hands means something different from saying that you can have everything you want. There may be some important things you think you want that aren't in the cards for you. What you want and what you don't want, in this sense, aren't terribly important. What is important is that you work deeply within yourself to understand the source and power of your life, and their natural direction – you could say, to understand your destiny.

I watch and participate with you in some specific and some general struggles that you go through, over things that you want and things that you don't want. Most of these struggles don't have anything to do with anything. Most of them are really this energy pulsating, changing patterns from within itself, emerging and re-emerging in these different expressions, and following its own course in its own way. This is why much of what you worry about and struggle with has an extraordinary way of working itself out, totally independent of how much you participate in it, how much you worry, or how much you struggle.

One of the terms you encounter a lot in different spiritual practices is the term "complete surrender." Complete surrender means at least two things. In the first place, it means having a trust so great that you could almost call it faith. What makes it different from faith is that, again and again, what you place your trust in demonstrates and proves its trustworthiness, so that you have evidence, experience, and a certainty of its reliability. Complete surrender is this kind of trust.

In the second place, in a very specific sense, complete surrender means learning to let go of your worries, your tensions, your attitudes, and your opinions. It means, at any given moment, being willing to release the mental and emotional structures with which you have confined the creative energy. So, in your daily struggles with all kinds of issues, the best thing you can do, again and again, is to release the mental and emotional framework through which you require the energy to work its way.

This means that you have to learn not to hold on to any feeling or idea or attitude that restricts the energy. Instead, allow it to assert itself from within you, to demonstrate its power, and to extend itself continuously – just as the ocean continuously extends itself in the form of the tides, re-arranging and re-shaping the shores of your conscious mind, as well as the landscape of your experience.

You have to learn to release your specific and general struggles over and over and over again. To shift analogies on you, you have to learn to surrender these stuggles into the fire of love – the fire of the creative energy of Life Itself within you. In this way, you allow the energy locked within you to be released. You open yourself for it to manifest itself within you, within your relationships, and in the field of your creative expression – which is your whole life.

In your practice, you find that the highest form of this experience really occurs as a meeting of spirits. It is a merging of hearts and minds that comes from deeply within us, that reaches deeply into us, and that nourishes and frees us in some deep and simple ways. The techniques that you practice help you sustain your concentration, so that you can also sustain a simple connection to this energy in a way that allows you to participate in it more and more deeply.

Over and over again you have to learn to appreciate the enormous creative capacity hidden within the energy. This is the creative capacity that sustains your body moment by moment, by which every aspect of you is both experienced and demonstrated, and that endlessly shows its power in countless ways in your life every day. And yet, people rarely trust it enough to open to it, to take time with it, or to allow it to demonstrate the depth of its capacity.

It may be that you feel the need to work through a lot of tensions, and that's all right. At the same time, in the context of your practice, it's really not the point. Your purpose here is not to work through tensions, but to learn to go beyond them – to experience a simple, pure flow. This flow – you can call it creative energy, nourishment, or love, if you want – allows you more and more to experience your own value, the extraordinary and sacred significance of your own life, and the endless, immeasurable, creative capacity hidden in that sacred life within you. It is in doing this that you ultimately become physically healed, emotionally well, and completely, spiritually fulfilled. What it comes down to is learning to trust in the creative flow of Life Itself.

INDEXES

ALPHABETICAL
INDEX OF TITLES

───

294

296

SUBJECT
INDEX

———

THE NITYANANDA INSTITUTE

The Nityananda Institute, headquartered in Cambridge, Massachusetts, is dedicated to the active practice of a spiritual life based on the teachings of Swami Chetanananda. The Institute (formerly the Rudrananda Ashram) is named for the Indian saint Bhagavan Nityananda of Ganeshpuri, who is its wellspring and inspiration. However, both Chetanananda and his *guru*, Swami Rudrananda (Rudi) were born Americans, and it is this rich fusion of East and West that gives the Institute its unique character. Even though Chetanananda's teaching is deeply rooted in the rich traditions of Tantrism, it is completely Western in expression. He speaks in the language of America, he is as familiar with rock and roll as with the Rig Veda; like Rudi before him, Chetanananda is the embodied proof that cultural affiliation is no barrier to the highest understanding.

The Institute has many facets: a community of over a hundred residents; a full schedule of hatha yoga classes; twice-daily meditation sessions (introductory course required); periodic workshops in meditation techniques, relaxation techniques, and health enhancement; programs of art, music, and dance; quarterly weekend Retreats; public Satsang programs on Sunday mornings; and a wide range of publications produced by its publishing house, *Rudra Press*.

ALSO FROM RUDRA PRESS

Video Tape

LILIAS! ALIVE WITH YOGA

"An instructional videocassette by America's best-known yoga teacher . . . informative, and non-intimidating to the beginner. A great gift for a loved one who is out of shape or non-physical and is looking for new ways to relax."

– Yoga Journal

With a warm and vital teaching style, Lilias Folan, star of the popular PBS-TV series "Lilias, Yoga and You" teaches us to stretch, strengthen and relax. Two 30-minute lessons include warm-ups, exercises for strength and flexibility, and a full range of yoga postures. Instructions in breath and relaxation to reduce stress and increase vitality!

Safe and easy to follow for practitioners of all ages. Music by Steven Halpern.

60 minutes, VHS or Beta $39.95

Audio Tapes

HATHA YOGA IN MOTION

Developed by the teaching staff of the Nityananda Institute, these hatha yoga audio tapes give balanced workouts for home practice. Two 30-minute practice sessions on each tape include warm-ups, asanas for strength and flexibility, and instruction in breath and relaxation.

Both tapes feature *vinyasa*, a graduated series of movement and breath which leads the student to a sense of ease and strength in the poses. By combining breath and movement, *vinyasa* practice also enables the student to develop a meditative understanding of hatha yoga. Each 60-minute tape includes a fold-out guide to the postures.

Beginner, Level 1 $9.95
Intermediate, Level 2 $9.95

308

Books

SPIRITUAL CANNIBALISM
by Rudi (Swami Rudrananda)

Originally published in 1973, *Spiritual Cannibalism* is an American spiritual classic. Rudi approached spiritual work with total intensity and dedication. In his direct, no-nonsense style, Rudi cuts through the fantasies of spirituality and directs us to the reality of spiritual work. Includes meditation instruction. This book is a must for every spiritual student.

New paperback edition $10.95

SONGS FROM THE CENTER OF THE WELL
by Swami Chetanananda

A wonderful collection of short, inspirational verse that speaks to the heart of living a conscious, spiritual life. Written from the unique perspective of an American spiritual master, *Songs* offers fresh insights on the discovery of the transcendental as we face the challenges and struggles of daily life.

Second edition, paper $6.95

NITYA SUTRAS: The Revelations of Nityananda from the Chidakash Gita
by M.U. Hatengdi and Swami Chetanananda

Nityananda's own words in an inspired translation of aphorisms recorded during the 1920s. In his terse, powerful style, Nityananda speaks of that inner awareness that is the goal of every spiritual student.

Informative introduction, commentaries, comprehensive glossary, and 20 rare photographs complete this remarkable volume.

Original paper $11.95

NITYANANDA: The Divine Presence
by M.U. Hatengdi

This book powerfully documents the life of one of India's greatest spiritual masters. Fascinating eye-witness stories and rare photographs trace Nityananda's life from the turn of the century to his *mahasamadhi* in 1961. These vivid stories compel us to suspend our rational assumptions as we meet one who is totally absorbed in the Absolute.

Original paper $10.95

TO ORDER

Call or write Rudra Press, P.O. Box 1973, Cambridge, MA 02238, (617) 576-3394.

When ordering by mail please include the following shipping charges with your payment: video/$3.00; books and tapes/$1.50 first item, $.50 each additional item. Thank you.

310